About the Author

Wim Dierckxsens is currently a research fellow at the Departamento Ecuménico de Investigación (DEI) in Costa Rica. Born in the Netherlands, and trained as a sociologist at the University of Brabant and as a demographer at the Sorbonne, he obtained his doctorate at the University of Nijmegen. In 1971 he moved to Central America, where he has lived ever since, holding a number of posts including working at the Latin American Centre for Demography and serving as director of postgraduate studies in economics at the Autonomous National University of Honduras. He is the author of a number of books in Spanish. These include:

Capitalismo y poblacion (1979) (translated into Dutch in 1980) (SUN, Nijmegen)

Formaciones Precapitalistas (1983)

Mercado de trabajo y politica economica en America Central (1990)

Globalizacion: Centroamerico y el Caribe en el nuevo orden (1992)

De la globalizacion a la Perestroika occidental (1994) (translated into English in 1995) (Tilburg University)

Critical Reception for this Book

Wim Dierckxsens's new book provides an excellent insight into the limited logic of neoliberalism, and paints a clear and systematic picture of the world's most likely future at the start of the new century if this doctrine is not abandoned.

Franz Hinkelammert, Central America

This is an excellent analysis from a third world perspective of the globalization process. It gives a clear and well-founded insight into the growing contradictions between the haves and the have-nots, and how this system may come to an end sooner than expected. The discussion of what the future could be and what options to neoliberalism exist is, without doubt, the most important contribution of this book.

The late Professor Gerrit Huizer, the Netherlands

The failing of the Multilateral Agreement on Investment (MAI) negotiations at the OECD in Paris in April 1998 and the huge protests against the World Trade Organization (WTO) round started in Seattle in December 1999 have shown not only the limits of neoliberalism and its ever deeper contradictions, but also the emergence of a new vision of building a more equal and fair global society. This book gives an excellent insight into the emergence of this process and its future.

François Houtart, Tricontinental Centre, University of Louvain, Belgium

The Limits of Capitalism

An approach to globalization without neoliberalism

Wim Dierckxsens

translated by Jayne Hutchcroft

Zed Books
LONDON • NEW YORK

The Limits of Capitalism: An approach to globalization without neoliberalism was first published by Zed Books Ltd, 7 Cynthia Street, London N1 9JF, UK and Room 400, 175 Fifth Avenue, New York, NY 10010, USA in 2000 in association with Inter Pares, 58 Arthur Street, Ottawa, Canada K1R 7B9.

Revised and updated from its original publication in Spanish under the title *Los Limites de un Capitalismo sin Ciudadania*, Coleccion Universitaria, Departamento Ecuménico de Investigación (DEI), Apartado Postal 390–2070, Sabanilla, San José, Costa Rica in 1998.

Distributed in the USA exclusively by St Martin's Press, Inc., 175 Fifth Avenue, New York, NY 10010, USA.

Cover designed by Andrew Corbett
Set in Monotype Dante by Ewan Smith, London
Printed and bound in Malaysia

A catalogue record for this book is available from the British Library

Library of Congress Cataloging-in-Publication Data

Dierckxsens, Wim.
[Limites de un capitalismo sin ciudadania, English]
The limits of capitalism: an approach to globalization without neoliberalism / Wim Dierckxsens; translated by Jayne Hutchcroft.
p. cm.
Includes bibliographical references and index.
ISBN 1-85649-868-9 (hb) –ISBN 1-85649-869-7 (pb)
1. International economic relations. 2. Globalization. 3. Capitalism. 4. Common good. I. Title.
HF1359.D53513 2000
337–dc21

00-063307

ISBN 1 85649 868 9 cased
ISBN 1 85649 869 7 limp

Contents

Figures and Tables

Figures

Tables

Acknowledgements

In preparing this book for publication, I have discussed ideas regarding the limits of capitalism-without-citizenry in the DEI (*Departamento Ecuménico de Investigación*), Costa Rica, in workshops and seminars, in local workshops throughout Central America and the Andean region, and in university courses and forums. This exchange has been my key to understanding the pulse of the times, and thus a new point of reference has emerged. For this reason, I am able to suggest in this current edition possible alternatives to neoliberalism in crisis. I am especially indebted to participants of DEI workshops who inspired and motivated me to analyse the present and to reflect on building a future with citizens. Without this grassroots support I would never have had the courage needed for this adventure.

Two people deserve special thanks for taking the time to discuss these ideas in depth with me since publication of the first edition. They are Dr Gerrit Huizer of the University of Nijmegen and Dr Lou Keune of the University of Brabant, both located in the Netherlands. They have constructively influenced this new version, which, though twice as long, has also been substantially restructured following their suggestions. Debate with Lou has been especially rich on concepts such as productive and nonproductive work, efficiency and vitality of the economy, and the concept of the Common Good. These discussions have helped clarify many ideas that were implied but not always clear in previous versions. Following suggestions by both of these supporters, additional empirical data have been included to strengthen the arguments presented in this study.

I would like to thank Ana Moya for her dedication and patience in reading and rereading the different stages of this latest version to improve the structure of the text. I also want to thank Mauricio Dierckxsens for his help in developing the many tables and graphs that accompany this text and, of course, Jayne Hutchcroft for the English translation of this version.

And finally, I cannot close without thanking Mariette Uitdewilligen, who has steadfastly encouraged me to follow this research through to its conclusion.

Introduction – Neoliberalism without Perspectives: Towards an Alternative Paradigm

This study aims to demonstrate that there are alternatives to neoliberal globalization. It proposes that there is a growing need for discussion and action to avoid this model becoming stuck in a dead end. Such a scenario gives rise to the historic possibility of constructing globalization without neoliberalization. Until now these issues have received little consideration. Important exceptions include Ramonet, 1997a; Forrester, 1996; Amin, 1996; Engelhard, 1996; Nell, 1996; and Roustang and Laville, 1996. Growing concern about an impending worldwide recession is leading to greater acceptance of debate on alternatives (Sachs, 1998), especially following the financial crises in Asia, Russia, and Brazil (Rohwer, 1998; Nocera, 1998; Fox, 1998).

Neoliberal theory is dominant and has claimed to be the unique successful paradigm (Engelhard, 1996: 550). In the face of this triumphant position, it has been difficult to construct other paradigms of economic theory without accentuating the cracks in the neoliberal model. This omnipresence and triumphant position make it all the more necessary to reveal neoliberalism's internal contradictions and cracks, beginning with the impending global recession, and particularly to demonstrate its temporal and finite nature.

There are different starting points in this analysis of neoliberal theory and its limits. For this project I have chosen an approach that first explains the transitory nature of neoliberalism in terms of its own limits. Second, the analytical strength of this approach can help to devise future scenarios. Third, it can shed light on possible alternatives, including globalization without neoliberalism. In other words, alternatives that are nonexclusive and citizen-based, a function of the Common Good, with a rationality rooted in the reproductive logic of the whole. The alternative proposed here cannot be predetermined, for it involves a series of abstractions requiring further work and debate in order to determine more concrete levels and possible actions.

The discussion on productive and nonproductive labour in Chapter 1 is the central axis of this study. Under the banner of neoliberalism, globalization directs investment towards nonproductive labour. With growing investment in the nonproductive sphere as determined by its content, capital tends to free itself by excluding the labour factor, and to realize virtual profits through speculative ventures. Labour relations become more flexible and allow a more intensive utilization. According to neoliberal logic, the rate of gain in the productive sphere will increase with the consequential return of investment to the same. Inasmuch as investment shows the opposite tendency, sooner or later the economic contraction that is threatening to engulf the world will become evident, along with the need for a new model of economic regulation. The difficulty in achieving this shift from the nonproductive (speculative) to the productive sphere under the neoliberal banner provides important clues for anticipating future alternative scenarios.

The concepts of productive and nonproductive labour are fundamental to any alternatives proposed from the outset of this study. These can be defined following two different perspectives. The first is based on the maximization of private profit aiming for economic efficiency that is well illustrated by current formal economics. The rationality directing this type of action is an abstract means–ends logic that disregards substantive aspects and ignores problems of a reproductive order (Hinkelhammert, 1995; Gutiérrez, 1997). The second begins with the reproduction of society as a whole and of the substantial part of the economy as explained by the father of economics, Adam Smith (1975). The former leads to the analysis of neoliberalism's internal logic while the latter leads to a better understanding of the need for economic regulation on a global scale.

In other words, productive labour can be analysed from two angles: by its form and by its content. This discussion is presented in the classical works of economic thought, including Marx, but is absent in neoclassical and neoliberal thought. By their form or prevailing social relationship, productive and nonproductive labour are seen from the perspective of individual capital. Productive labour is defined here in relation to capital. Although the physiocrats erroneously thought that only agricultural labour was productive, they correctly postulated the idea that from the capitalist point of view, productive labour is that which creates surplus value (Quesnay, 1958). Adam Smith arrived at this same point, which is the heart of the matter, by defining productive labour as labour exchanged directly for capital, pointing explicitly to the social relationship (Smith, 1975).

Neoclassicals in general, and neoliberals in particular, see productive labour defined by its form as the only possibility. For them, debate on this topic has lost all substance. Boundary lines are found within the monetary economy: is labour for the market the only productive labour according to the logic of profit maximization? Is labour for the market that does not follow this logic also productive, or is non-mercantile monetary labour in the redistributive state sphere also productive? The neoliberal approach tends to limit the concept to the former. All labour outside this dominant social relationship ultimately is considered nonproductive and can even be seen as an unnatural labour relationship that should be restricted. Therefore, neoliberals see all activities developed by the state that could be undertaken for profit by private enterprise as unnatural and subject to restrictive measures. As Hayek states (1992: 328):

> The question of what any specific agency has the right to do or what degree of government power it is allowed to exercise is often known as the discretionary issue. It is obvious that not all government actions can be limited by fixed rules, but ... it is probably necessary that bureaucratic organizations be limited by norms ... since they lack that efficiency test inherent to the nature of business's profit-making.

Since the natural perspective of neoclassical economists is to view things according to their form, they do not distinguish between productive and nonproductive labour according to content or substance. From this perspective, it seems unimportant whether investments are made in the productive or nonproductive spheres when defined by content. From the standpoint of prevailing social relationships all labour exchanged directly for capital is productive, so the substance of labour is unimportant. By not recognizing the nonproductive nature of labour by-its-content, it is impossible to understand how neoliberal

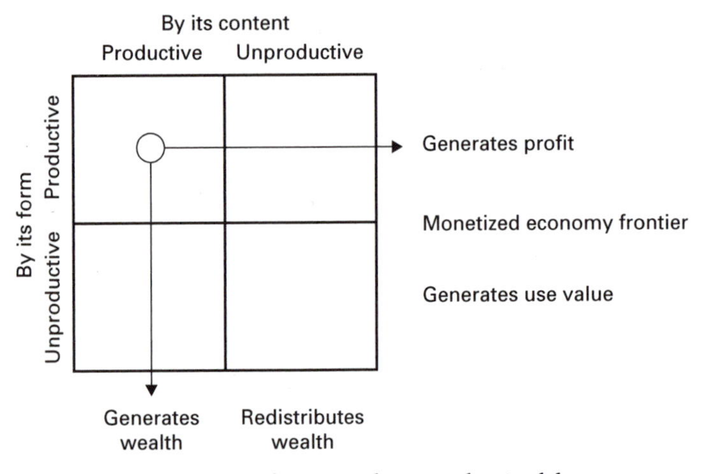

Figure Int.1 Productive and nonproductive labour

economies can stagnate. When everything is governed more and more exclusively by private enterprise's search for profit maximization, efficiency at a microsum level leads to progressive economic stagnation; that is, to limited reproduction of the whole. As investments increasingly become more nonproductive by-their-content, efficiency of the parts can expand, but only at the expense of the system that it tends to destroy. It threatens not only nature and human life, but also the very life of the system itself.

From the perspective of content, that is to say, abstracting the social relationship in which it is realized, real or materialized labour that acts on the social form of the prevailing production regime does not create wealth. This labour entails false production costs that are paid through the redistribution of existing wealth (Marx, 1974: II, 125–8). Regardless of the social relationship within which it originates, only labour that generates material or nonmaterial use value is productive according to content. It is not important to this discussion that in our society this wealth primarily appears in the form of goods that are often produced in a relationship between labour and capital (Marx, 1971: I, 55, 190).

Productive labour can be better understood using a matrix model. Productive labour defined by its content indicates the creation of wealth, while nonproductive labour indicates its redistribution. This perspective requires analysis of the reproductive sphere as a whole.

The other axis of the matrix (see Figure Int.1) indicates productive labour by-its-form. All labour that generates profit for capital is productive by-its-form, and all labour that is unprofitable is not productive for capital. This perspective is rooted in capital's distinctive interests. From this angle, the whole is constituted by the sum total of private interests. A matrix for interpreting different combinations of efficiency and vitality on these two axes can be shaped along the lines of the two perspectives used to analyse productive labour. The concept of productive labour following the two axes of vitality and efficiency is central to this study, and is developed in Chapter 1.

It is difficult at this time to interpret productive labour beyond its form. We are accustomed to viewing things from the perspective of their social forms. In our social accounting, only labour that acquires some monetary expression is considered to be productive (Gough, 1978: 92). Any labour performed on content that lacks a monetary expression, such as domestic and volunteer labour, is not included in social bookkeeping regardless of its contribution to the reproduction of production conditions as a whole.

It is often the case that labour affecting the form – commerce, banking, insurance, the stock market, real estate, and legal property transfers, among others – that functions according to the dominant model, in other words, as private enterprise seeking to maximize profits, is a source of greater benefits than the profits made in the productive sector. For reasons we will examine later, this labour that is seen as nonproductive by-its-content is more lucrative than productive labour by-its-content. In spite of the profits generated by nonproductive labour by-its-content (such as speculative labour), its investments and expenditures represent false costs (*faux frais*) of social production. The distinction between surplus value and profit (ibid.: 101) aptly expresses the difference between benefits obtained in the productive sphere (productive profits) and nonproductive profits (commercial, banking and speculative profits, among others). The latter exist only through the redistribution of profits generated in the productive sphere. This means that growing investment in the nonproductive sector entails increasing redistribution of wealth and surplus value, a decreasing average rate of gain, and thus stagnation of the economy as a whole (Marx, 1974: I, 244–54).

Historical analyses with greater prospective analytical capabilities are possible by using the categories of productive and nonproductive labour. In this way, it is possible to analyse the parasitic subordination of noncapitalist forms of labour to commercial and usury capital in the transition from feudalism to capitalism. During this transitional period, productive labour by-its-content (artisanal and agricultural labour) was subordinated to commercial and usury capital, just as productive labour by-its-content now tends to be subordinated to financial capital (Dierckxsens, 1979: 91–117). This same category of productive labour also sheds light on the economic stagnation in antiquity, as shown in previous studies of the Roman empire (Dierckxsens, 1983). That empire's permanent warfare in search of replacement slaves is a historic example of the redistribution of human and material resources using violence. As the empire expanded, the costs of war became increasingly higher compared with its benefits. This resulted in the progressive need to emancipate the slaves and a gradual transition towards other relations of production (ibid.: 149–54). The category of (non)productive labour also helps to distinguish the periods of prosperity (collective labour in irrigation or terracing) from those of crisis (prolonged collective labour for religion or war) in the ancient societies of Egypt, the Incas, Mayas or Aztecs (ibid.: 84–93).

In more recent times, the category of (non)productive labour illuminates the unequal abilities of the former USSR and the USA to support defence spending during the Cold War. Although they maintained similar levels of defence spending, the USSR's gross domestic product was only about half that of the USA. This hindered the development of its civil economy and led to the weak development of consumption. The acceleration of the arms race in both countries during the 1980s led to the limited reproduction of its economy and the later disintegration of the Soviet bloc (Dierckxsens, 1992: 101–13).

More recently under neoliberalism, progressive investment in nonproductive sectors has led to a loss of vitality in the world economy. The historical perspective implicit in the category of (non)productive labour examined in the studies mentioned above gives rise to greater analytical capabilities to devise future scenarios that can result from an eventually besieged neoliberalism. This in turn helps to construct alternatives.

Beginning in the late 1960s and early 1970s, the world economy has shown symptoms of a declining growth rate. This coincided with the oil crisis that at first was seen as an explanation of the situation. Today almost no one attributes this decline in economic growth to the oil crisis (Engelhard, 1996: 61). Engelhard claims that this loss of dynamism is now primarily attributed to the growing cost of innovation. These costs were apparent from the onset of the oil crisis, but intensified even as oil prices dropped again.

Innovation loses its purpose within capitalism when it no longer contributes to increasing the rates of profit. Profit rates tend to drop when a given percentage of growth in labor's productivity requires a greater than proportional increase in the cost of innovation (Engelhard, 1996: 63). The rising cost of innovation, beyond the growth in productivity, results from competition. Competition demands accelerated depreciation; in other words, an increasingly rapid rate of innovation that in turn raises the cost of innovations. Labour productivity's growth is more difficult as the cost of innovation increases. The resulting drop in the profit rates in the productive sphere stimulates capital flight towards nonproductive sectors.

By fleeing the productive sectors, accumulation is not based on real valuation of capital. The size of the pie tends to grow more slowly. When the pie does not grow, accumulation is possible only through progressive concentration of existing wealth using a dual approach that will be explained in Chapter 2. Monetarism, or the decree of purely monetary accumulation, essentially allows for the possibility of accumulation of 'unemployed capital' that no longer uses (productive) labour as it gambles on the prospect of more intensive future exploitation of that labour. Capital accumulates monetary wealth without a corresponding use of labour in the productive sphere. By temporarily not using labour, capital implements a policy of exclusion and flexibility culminating in the progressive concentration of existing wealth. Following Thurow, this represents a declaration of 'war on labour' by capital (Thurow, 1996: 180).

In Chapter 2 we examine the trend since the 1970s of the flight of investments to nonproductive sectors. This has led to slower growth in the global pie and has caused it to be divided up to compensate these ever larger nonproductive investments. This leads to lower average profits for social capital. It is in this context of decreasing average profits that what Thurow has called the 'Economic World War' for the same market breaks out (Thurow, 1992). The strategy involves strengthening competitive market positions to capture a larger market segment and a greater portion of existing wealth, rather than stimulating growth via investments in productive areas to generate new wealth. In this context it is important to understand the mergers and acquisitions policies that constitute the majority of investments in the world today.

Mergers and acquisitions policies raise the expectation that the strongest will triumph in the world; in other words, the large transnational corporations. The stock market, where the stronger companies are traded, is an expression of this expectation. Stock transactions are not always made with the money from savings, that is, with existing wealth. Over the years an inverted pyramid of credit built on growing debt rather than on savings has led to stocks selling for much higher prices than their real market value. Such increases reflect an expectation of future profits and thus feed future speculation. The stakes set on transnational corporations that are big winners in the stock market and the resulting credit are much higher than economic growth or the growth of real profits they generate. The profits nominally received from the transactions are removed from the real economy. As the credit spiral grows accumulation becomes more of a virtual reality. Sooner or later, if investment is unable to reconnect with production, there could be a global financial crisis such as the one currently on the horizon.

In Chapter 3, we examine how investment in recent decades has gradually abandoned the production sphere, making a global financial crisis an even greater possibility. As stock prices plummet, this crisis would become neoliberalism's trial by fire, even for the largest transnational corporations.

The financial crisis in Asia should be seen not as an isolated event but as a dispute over a market that does not have room for all transnational corporations. The cause of this crisis is not in Asia, Russia or Latin America, where monetary instability is most evident. Rather, it is caused by the battle among large transnational corporations for a slowly expanding world market that is in danger of shrinking. A shrinking market gradually demonstrates that there is no longer room for everyone, not even for all transnationals. As a result, competitive businesses use a strategy of mergers and acquisitions to corner large parts of the existing market.

Chapter 3 also describes how Asian markets protected themselves from external investment. This led to an imbalance of direct foreign investment between East and West, which in turn created a trade imbalance. These imbalances greatly intensified the economic market crisis between East and West. The destabilization of Asian currencies since mid-1997, often caused by external speculative mechanisms and resulting in the subordination of these countries to recent structural adjustment policies, can be understood within this context. 'Caging the Tigers' leaves more room for participation by the winners from the West. Consequently, the international stock market was expected to become more Westernized and more North Americanized. Apparently the Western stock market could indefinitely postpone a crash, at the expense of the recession in the East. The result for the global economy as a whole has been an overall loss of dynamism. Removing the spark from the Asian economy's motor has taken the energy out of the world economy as well. Under such circumstances, recessions in the world are now more frequent than recoveries. The increasing threat of recession is illustrated by the Russian crisis. Broader recession increasingly brings about a contraction of global demand, thus increasing the risk of overproduction and consequent deflation. Deflation brings falling profit rates and even disturbs the investment climate in the West. Instead of subsiding, the danger of a worldwide financial crisis actually increases.

A worldwide financial breakdown challenges neoliberal economics, for it shows that crises strike even the largest transnational corporations; in other words, the Common Bad becomes evident. Is a worldwide financial crisis at all avoidable? Is there room for the global stock market to recuperate? Space still remains for the casino economy. Agreements such as an international interest reduction (Sachs, 1998: 21) could help postpone a general crisis, but this will be increasingly difficult to avoid altogether.

Financial liberalization is one of the measures that helped accelerate the international financial crisis (ibid.: 22). The Multilateral Agreement on Investment (MAI) is a recent but failed attempt to liberalize the flow of capital. This agreement promoted investment in other countries (including speculative investments) as well as the integral withdrawal of ensuing profits. Eventually it was meant to regulate disputes among nation-states over issues of foreign investment. The strengthening of economic blocs is another mechanism that has been progressively used to concentrate wealth in favour of transnational corporations, but this has reduced the vitality of the world economy as a whole. With this concentration, global demand contracts and real profits fall for even the most successful companies. Future prospects become negative. Even the largest companies have difficulty maintaining their real profits when demand contracts and oversupply leads to global deflation. This gradually frustrates the expectations of future profits. In the long run it is difficult to avoid a global financial crisis.

Concentration of wealth occurs not only when businesses are competing for a nonexpanding market, but also, at the same time, in the contentious realm of capital and labour. This is shown in Chapter 4. Competition in a nonexpanding market encourages the strengthening of positions within that market by mergers, acquisitions, publicity, marketing, and so forth. These investments do not lead to growth. Instead they strengthen the world's wealthiest regions, where the most successful transnational corporations of the various sectors are located. The neoliberal model seems to function in these countries or regions. Simultaneously, however, this tendency contributes to a growing differentiation and exclusion in other wealthy countries and areas of the world. The levels of exclusion in the peripheral areas go without mention. The result for the global economy as a whole is a relative and even absolute loss of employment opportunities. Full employment ceases to be a guiding value. The trend is to protect the general employment situation, even though this could lead to growing structural unemployment and to less stable and lower-paying jobs with less social security.

Progressive exclusion means a loss in acquired rights, that is, a loss in citizenship. The welfare state tends to break down in a deregulated market economy, intervening less and less in matters of economic and social rights. People tend to blame the state in their demands and struggles, but the state's own sphere has been reduced by the market. Following Forrester (1997: 20), we ask what the future holds for citizens in the wake of progressive exclusion. What would happen should democracy disappear? Would there not be a risk of formulating the excess (that in turn would grow relentlessly)? What would happen if the 'merit' on which the right to life and rights in general increasingly depend were judged and administered by an authoritarian regime?

> In a democracy no one would dare state that life is not a right and that there are too many living things. But would anyone do this under a totalitarian regime? Has it not been done already? (Forrester, 1997: 32)
>
> Indifference is appalling. It is the biggest part ... and that indifference can be seen as support for certain regimes. (ibid.: 49)
>
> Exaggerations? That is what everyone says when there is still time to realize that harming one hair on the head could portend that the worst was yet to come. And that crimes against humanity are always crimes against humanity. (ibid.: 154)

As will be described in Chapter 4, this progressive exclusion taking place throughout the world can be expected to produce a variety of future scenarios. Exclusion means the loss of jobs in the labour market along with a loss of social rights, of citizenship, and therefore it is an identity crisis. Delegitimizing this progressive exclusion can also lead to demands for a society that has room for everyone, which implies questioning the very roots of the exclusionary system. The response to exclusion can lead to questioning the legitimacy of exclusion without questioning the society that created it. But this does not confront the roots of the problem; quite the contrary. One model of exclusion, that of the market, is substituted for another, that of belonging or not to certain communities (racial, national, cultural, etc.). It is in this context that burgeoning xenophobia, the resurgence of nationalism in the world and conflicts among cultures, are examined in Chapter 5.

The grassroots struggle for nonexclusion could eventually overlap with the fight of big capital for nonexclusion. Historically this has been the case with fascism. Forrester states that fascism was not expected to develop out of the crisis of the 1930s, and that there are no guarantees it would never happen again (Forrester, 1997). In a world that has room for fewer and fewer transnationals, not excluding citizens from an economic bloc depends on not excluding its transnational corporations. In the struggle for nonexclusion, Huntington (1993: 27–9) claims that transnational corporations are benefiting more from the conflict among cultures and civilizations than from nationalism. Nationalism provides very limited opportunity for the interests of transnational capital. Nationalism as such no longer represents a unifying banner for furthering transnational capital. He suggests (ibid.) that the threat posed to Western culture by the rise of Eastern culture could kindle a conflict between civilizations. This is apparent in the financial assault on Asian currencies and the subordination of these economies to structural adjustment programmes that in turn open them to foreign investment and 'caging the Tigers'. The assault on Asian currencies indicates that this war is more and more being waged in the economic arena. This predicts a Westernizing or North Americanizing of globalization. It is in this sense that Engelhard suggests World War III has already begun (Engelhard, 1997).

Since the start of the Asian crisis, International Monetary Fund (IMF) economic projections (IMF 1998: 1) have shown a marked contraction in the growth rates of Southeast Asian economies. Latin American growth rates were expected to fall. Among the world powers a clear decline in the Japanese economy was anticipated in 1998. The strict adjustment policies in Asia have not invigorated the global economy, which grew almost 1% less in 1998 than predicted prior to the Asian crisis (IMF, 1998: 3). The Russian crisis further underscored the negative forecasts for the world economy. A progressive contraction of demand is expected to contribute to falling profit rates for the most successful large transnational corporations. This will only further the worldwide financial crisis.

The only way the world economy can recover from such a crisis is to give priority to the whole rather than saving the parts, as will be explained in Chapter 6. This is possible only with worldwide economic regulation. The demand for globalization without neoliberalism, however, does not necessarily represent an alternative that would subordinate efficiency to the worldwide Common Good. It is not easy to shift from values centred on individual interests to those centred on the vitality of the whole, as that requires some fundamental value changes.

There is strong historical precedent showing that a (neo)liberal approach will not resolve the crisis. The panic spawned by a depression can radicalize the struggle for involvement at any cost. Neither does this response return the focus to the Common Good; quite the contrary. Awareness of the limitations of a neoliberalism that lacks real perspectives will in all probability lead to a search for economic regulation that is aimed at reconciling private and transnational interests with vitalization. Basically that is understood to be growth with involvement. One means of achieving this could be through an aggregate global demand and worldwide involvement policies. In this way, private accumulation could continue without being subjected to the global Common Good. This would be a type of global neo-Keynesianism, requiring some sort of world state regulator.

The primary task of this global neo-Keynesianism would be to regulate the world economy in which transnational corporations operate. This task would not be the responsibility of any one nation-state; it would require worldwide regulation. In this regard, the growing discussion on regulating speculation is a healthy sign (Nell, 1996; Martin and Schumann, 1996; Sachs, 1998). However, discussion going beyond global financial regulation is scarce (Petrella, 1996; Roustang and Laville, 1996; Rifkin, 1997). Their proposals involve the deficiency of competitive advantages, and that revitalization implies a reversal along the lines of efficiency. They propose the need for a new social contract, but at a worldwide rather than a national level.

Viable solutions are unlikely to be found through global neo-Keynesian interventions. Could an aggregate demand with global employment policies be achieved by the intervention of a sort of nation-state? Even if such a project were successful, it would be difficult to regulate resource distribution in a market system governed by profit maximization. Aggregate demand achieved through global regulation that stimulates technology development would merely reinforce the trend towards more idle capacity and depreciation exceeding the rise in labour productivity. This would result in lower profit rates.

It is not enough just to guarantee the scale of demand. It is equally important to define its composition (Nell, 1996: 61). A visible hand regulating depreciation and investments is needed to resolve the downward trend in profit rates. As will be explained in Chapter 6, such intervention is possible only when it is simultaneously introduced throughout the world. Globally regulated depreciation would give new impetus to technological development, with greater conservation of natural resources and redistribution of global income. This regulation represents direct intervention in economic rationality, thus subordinating efficiency to the vitality of the system as a whole.

Efforts to implement worldwide neo-Keynesian economic regulation could lead to changes in economic rationality and its subordination to a visible hand on a global scale. Sooner or later the need to favor vitality over efficiency will become evident. The latter qualitatively modifies economic rationality, thus changing its very essence. Any future regulation, in my opinion, will lead to that qualitative leap in relations of production since there is no real possibility of making investment return to the productive sphere without giving priority to economic vitality. In other words, productive forces have reached the limits of their development potential under existing economic rationality. According to this perspective, only with great difficulty can other paradigms emerge. Neoliberalism dogmatically props up prevailing rationality.

In this context, progressive sectors are faced with the truly historic challenge of helping construct a new society on a global scale that is guided by the Common Good. Such efforts can be characterized as globalization from below. On the other hand, these sectors are poorly prepared to deal with globalization that is based on the Common Good for citizens throughout the world. This process supposes a discussion that is just beginning (Petrella, 1996; Huizer, 1996; Amin, 1996; Laville, 1997). The search for global economic vitality would occur at the expense of efficiency but without suppressing it altogether. This involves a major reorientation of the economy towards the Common Good (Engelhard, 1996). Such a shift would entail a change in values, a new ethics of solidarity and a new type of citizen to meet this challenge.

Globalization based on a worldwide Common Good begins by focusing on the reproduction of human life and of nature, in other words, the citizenry as a whole. This reproduction is not subordinated to the logic of the efficiency of the parts. In the last instance, efficiency of the parts leads to inefficiency on the level of the whole by exclusion or waste of resources on a global level. Efficiency of the whole means working with all human and natural resources, with no wastefulness or exclusion in the system and without needing to achieve maximum efficiency of the parts (Nell, 1996: 97).

The shift in priorities from efficiency to vitality invariably involves a risk of centralization of power, as was the case after real socialism eradicated market relations. This response included the radical substitution of the total market for the total plan. Agreement with the plan and those defining it replaces absolute agreement with the market. The shift can be gradual, without essential change from one perspective to another. Such was the case with Keynesianism. Vitality and efficiency were reconciled in the Keynesian world although efficiency was never subordinate to vitality. This reconciliation ended in the 1970s with the decline of profit rates. Absolute deregulation was introduced under neoliberalism to preserve profits. As these limits are reached, the shift to reregulation of the world economy requires a gradual but very real subordination of efficiency to the citizenry.

1

Efficiency versus the Common Good

The Economy and the Common Good

Productive forces in the market economy have unquestionably reached unprecedented levels of development that can, in principle, provide for the well-being of the entire world. We live in a period of globalization of the market economy that at the same time leads to exclusion on a global scale. We ask ourselves why globalization and generalization of efficiency have led to a society that promotes economic stagnation and exclusion. Clearly the unregulated market economy governed by private interests is disconnected from the Common Good. An invisible hand separates it from the sum total of completely unregulated competing private interests. What is the Common Good? If it is not the sum of private interests, then how is it defined?

> The Common Good consists of the fact that the persons or groups comprising a society have interests that cannot be reduced to the sum of individual interests. (Engelhard, 1996: 459)

'There are things of interest to everyone that surpass the private interests of each' (Arrow, 1963 in Engelhard, 1996: 456). As a rule, the state assumes common interests; however, it cannot escape the influence of private ones (Engelhard, 1996: 460). Directing the economy in function of the Common Good necessarily entails economic regulation where private interests are mediated by the interests of all citizens, but in case of contradiction are subordinate to them. Democratic political management is essential to any such regulation.

In the Keynesian period there was mediation between private interest and the Common Good as well as efficiency and vitality, but in cases of irreconcilable conflict private interest prevailed over interests of citizens. This reversal of priorities gives rise to vitality and the Common Good. This is a case of economic rationality in function of the citizenry where private interests and efficiency still exist, but are subordinated to the interests of the whole. The Common Good is thus an economic rationality in function of citizens, in which they enjoy democratic participation. However, as economic rationality based on private interest continues to depart from the Common Good, a market ethic based on private interest expands at the expense of a solidarity ethic grounded in participatory democracy.

A concept of the economy that incorporates both politics and ethics is essential to any critical understanding of how the free play of the market abandons the Common Good in this age of globalization. Political economy is the only theoretical approach that clearly deals with this conjunction. In the current view, there is a separation between ethics and economic sciences. Critical theories denouncing the irrationality of the current economic order and claiming that it continues to stray from the Common Good are proclaimed to be outside the realm of science, belonging instead to that of ethics, ideology, politics, and so on. Economics no longer sees itself as political economy – although in essence it really is – and political economy is no longer considered science.

A perspective that segregates economics and ethics, or at least excludes them from scientific debate, hampers real opposition. This separation has not always existed.

> Contrary to popular ideas, the economic sciences arise from a moral debate (Hume, Smith) which was more a political problem than a theoretical issue. (Gutiérrez, 1997: 18)

When liberal thought first began economics and political economy were seen to go hand in hand. Both dealt with substantivist economics grounded in the reproductive logic of capital, and they were inseparable. Their segregation began with the neoclassics. To separate ethics from economics the market needed to appear to be a natural product of history, a self-referenced system, and the means of general well-being and progress (ibid.: 20). The triumph of formalist economics over the substantive approach is accompanied by a change in the relationship between the economy and ethics.

The separation of ethics and politics from economics begins with Adam Smith and his work leading to the shift from substantive to formal economics. In *The Theory of Moral Sentiments*, Smith (1975) claims that individual private interests are articulated in the market as if an invisible hand were directing the market towards the Common Good (see Gutiérrez, 1997: 20). Once this notion was accepted,

> economic thought could dispense with any concept of needs, and enter into the infinite universe of preferences and desires, the pillar of abstract neoclassical systemic determinism … After Smith, economic theory assumed the market was the natural medium to regulate economic activity, and it was able to become a formal, quantitative and systemic science, unconcerned with ethical or moral issues. (ibid.)

After Smith economics abandons the theory of reproduction as well as substantive economics and its discussions of economic rationality. Formal economics 'dispenses with substantive concerns, and does not see problems of a reproductive sort or declares them to be external'. How society reproduces life within the framework of certain social relations of production is not considered a human creation, but rather an external reality (ibid.: 17.22). Consequently, any challenge to prevailing economic rationality is considered nonscientific and, therefore, external to economic debate.

Challenges to the neoliberal model are gradually gaining ground. There is growing evidence that the invisible hand does not guide the sum total of competing private interests towards the Common Good. This is increasingly apparent in the destruction of nature and the generalization of exclusion and poverty, but it does not yet signal a crisis for large capital. That will occur only when profits are endangered, such as in the Asian and especially Russian crises.

> The Common Good is destroyed to the degree that all human activity is submitted to calculations of utility. The generalization of these calculations results in the violation of the Common Good. (Hinkelhammert, 1997: 35)

When calculations of utility are endangered in the short term, there is growing concern for profits in the long term. Long-term calculations necessarily lead to an analysis of reproduction, which demonstrates the need to examine the movement of capital as a whole and reveals the contradictions between private and collective interests. The rationality of regulation and of the free play of the market can be compared using this reproductive logic to reveal alternatives favouring citizens and serving the lives of real human beings with needs – in other words, alternatives favouring vitality.

Economic rationality based on the Common Good arises from the totality and not from private interests. The economic intervention it requires does not yet entail abolishing the market system. Getting rid of that system would mean losing a way to mediate between private interests and the Common Good, and quickly lead to substitution of the total single market by an absolute centralized plan. This shift from one form of totalization to another – from the total market to the total plan – is an unintended consequence. Citizens have no participation in the formulation of this plan, and as a result it tends not to serve them.

The economic rationality arising from the Common Good requires regulation, but not of just any kind. In these terms, Keynesianism provided regulation of the economy's efficiency and vitality, without the former being subordinated to the latter. Rather than subordinating private interests to collective interests, Keynesian regulation used intentional mediation between private interests and the Common Good to extend efficiency in the long term.

This Keynesian regulation was exhausted in the 1970s, when efficiency began to show signs of retreat. Since then the free play of the market has gradually been restored. The cracks in neoliberalism have become more and more apparent as efficiency has collided with capital's primary interests. The search for private profit undermines its realization at the level of the totality; there is across-the-board loss. It will then be the historic moment to demand regulation that subordinates private interests to the Common Good.

Productive and Nonproductive Labour and the Common Good

The global world is subjected to the lineal means–ends calculations of business and the increasingly unmediated maximization of private profit. Efficiency or productive labour by-form becomes the highest value. What is efficient is good and necessary, and is above question.

Efficiency in the private sphere is essential to survival in the market, especially an all-encompassing one. Efficiency applies to all sectors, regardless of the involved labour's content.

The sum total of growing efficiency on the private level can, and in this era of globalization actually does, result in a loss of 'efficiency' on the level of the whole. What seems to be rational from the point of view of private interests is actually irrational and 'inefficient' for the whole, that is, for citizens in general. Efficiency on the level of the whole is known as vitality. The contradiction between private-level efficiency and the loss of vitality for the whole can occur at any moment in the history of capitalism, but most clearly when larger amounts of capital are invested in nonproductive sectors.

As seen in the Introduction, the concepts of productive and non-productive labour can be looked at from two possible angles: that of the form or social relationship, and that of content. These concepts are essential to understanding the two central facets of efficiency and vitality. Different authors have continued the analyses of this topic by Adam Smith and Karl Marx, including Altvater and Feerkhuizen (1978); Baran and Sweezy (1966); Gough (1978); and Fiorito (1974). Ian Gough's analysis, in my opinion, represents the most successful effort based on Marx's work in *Capital* and *Theories of Surplus Value* to integrate these concepts of productive labour by-content and by-form.

Productive labour by-content makes an abstraction of prevailing social relationships that is crucial to any comparative study of society. In the abstract, productive labour is that which creates material or spiritual wealth; however, defined according to content it produces services to satisfy needs as well as tangible wealth. Tourism and entertainment are as productive in this context as agriculture and industry.

Productive labour that creates surplus value is exclusive to the capitalist mode of production (Gough, 1978: 79). For Marx, this was a historically specific concept, making it important to distinguish productive labour under capitalism from productive labour in general.

All human production takes place within social relationships, and in a market economy these are expressed in monetary terms. We can distinguish between mercantile and nonmercantile monetary relationships. Capitalist relationships are mercantile but they are also more than that. Not all production is distributed in the form of commodities.

There is also nonmercantile distribution – via the state. Monetarized products distributed in this manner, for example through taxes, are included in national bookkeeping. Nonmonetarized production, on the other hand, is for personal consumption. It is neither mercantile nor monetary. Home production for personal consumption is a good example.

Although they are not one and the same, capitalist relations require mercantile relations in order to function, leading also to changes in the social significance of productive labour. From a mercantile perspective productive labour is that which creates use values that find their equivalent, or exchange value, in the market. Use values kept for personal consumption and not transformed into commodities are excluded here, as is often the case with domestic labour. Productive labour in the framework of capitalist relations is even narrower, including only wage labour that produces profits for capital.

The same productive labour by-content can be productive or non-productive by-form depending on prevailing social relationships. A factory worker who produces a commodity – food, clothes, etc. – is productive from any angle. However, as a government employee she would not be productive for capital, since it is considered a cost even though it is a monetarized activity. This leads to a perception of government inefficiency in spite of its eventual effectiveness in certain productive activities. The self-employed woman who sells her goods on the street is productive in the market economy, but not from capital's perspective. Although these goods are distributed commercially and can even generate profits, this retail labour is not productive for capital. If she made the same items for her own family's use that labour would not be monetarized, and she would no longer be productive in those terms. It is not included in the social bookkeeping. Domestic labour can lead to greater vitality in terms of reproduction and can be very productive by-content, but raising children, and cooking and sewing for the family, are considered nonproductive labour for the monetary economy.

In the context of monetary relations anything not quantifiable is not included as social wealth. Thus, nature and domestic labour, as well as a significant part of existing social wealth when defined according to content – that is, from the perspective of the whole – are not taken into account. This is the basis of contempt for unpaid labour and indifference towards the environment. Domestic labour plays an important part in the reproduction of life itself and thus contributes to the system's vitality. Labour not included in social bookkeeping is nonproductive from the perspective of capital. Research on the reproductive logic of capital and of the labour force – relating lower replacement prospects with women's income levels in the job market – have made important steps towards explaining unpaid labour's role (Harrison, 1974; Dierckxsens, 1979; Singer, 1980).

It is similar with nonproduced wealth. The natural environment constitutes wealth when defined according to its content, but not when defined according to its form. As long as natural resources are not quantified and included in bookkeeping this wealth is not taken into account and does not even exist in economic terms. According to Leff (1986: 38): 'Until recently, the relative abundance of natural resources in relation to capitalist accumulation's needs concealed the importance of ecological reproduction and of ecosystems' primary productivity in the process of capital reproduction.'

When comparing productive and nonproductive labour by-form or by-content the perspective of one does not necessarily coincide with the other. However, since dominant social relations are portrayed as natural and 'eternal', the concept of productive labour defined according to its dominant form appears to be an 'absolute' concept, using Gough's terms (1978: 78). Thus, for neoclassic economists productive labour appears simultaneously as both form and content.

From this angle it is difficult to detect why greater efficiency in nonproductive sectors should lead to increased nonproductive investment and thus greater stagnation and exclusion. Extreme efficiency based on increasingly aggressive competition among private interests therefore leads to greater separation from the Common Good and towards the Common Bad. When private interests and the laws of the market are taken to such extremes that they oppose the citizens and even threaten profits – efficiency itself – we can speak of the Common Bad. Not even capital can find a way out of this situation. This is precisely what occurs in extreme neoliberal economies.

Companies specializing in nonproductive activities by-their-content that are very lucrative by-their-form – such as stock market ventures, and currency or real estate speculation – are portrayed as productive. Altvater and Feerkhuizen observed that:

> In the bourgeois system of production, all labour that preserves or increases its base – capital – can be defined as productive, while labour that is not necessary within this system is seen as nonproductive ... As a result when calculating national income ... all revenues are seen as portions of the 'big pie', of the social product. (1978: 8)

Neoclassical economists give equal weight to the fruits of production and redistribution, resulting in the need to identify nonproductive labour defined according to its content.

Mercantile and monetary relations are central to capitalism, even though they and the labour involved do not create wealth: 'Circulation is only one phase of the reproduction process, but it produces no value and thus no surplus value' (Gough, 1978: 87).

The distinction between production and commercialization is not always clear, but the latter has to do with the formal transfer of products. The primary difference between production and circulation or realization 'is found in activities that are essential to production in general and to mercantile production in particular' (Marx cited in ibid.: 88).

Transportation-related labour involves spatial transfer that does not depend on mercantile relations, but instead concerns production in general. It involves content but not form.

In contrast, the act of buying and selling stocks or real estate, for example, and subsequent notary services, represent a formal transfer that creates no wealth whatsoever, no matter how many times that stock or real estate is transferred. It may represent juicy profits for intermediaries but in broader terms for the social whole it involves redistribution rather than creation of wealth. A private company may find it more productive to make its profits in the financial rather than the productive sphere, and thus increase its individual capital. On the whole, however, capital's tendency to retreat to nonproductive sectors does not create new wealth: 'Profits from trade, banking, and insurance capital can only be made through complex distribution processes that transfer a part of surplus value to them' (Altvater and Feerkhuizer, 1978: 36).

Instead of stimulating the economy, distribution actually reduces rates of accumulation (ibid.: 40). Increased investment in this sphere can lead to economic stagnation and even contraction. Thus at times of increasing nonproductive investment, the sum of private interests and those of capital in general are very different.

For individual capital all labour that generates profits is productive, regardless of the type of labour. Fire insurance uses revenues from premium payments merely to redistribute or socialize losses among the whole of society. For individual capital in this sector it can be a source of higher than average profits, but when defined by its content – on the level of society in general – it is only redistribution of losses. It helps avoid disarticulating economic activities and indirectly contributes to continued extended reproduction. It furthers the Common Good but is still a nonproductive enterprise (see ibid.: 7).

During severe economic crises commercialization of goods and services, and especially of money, takes on a life of its own, breaking away from the productive sphere through speculation and clearly demonstrating its sterility for economic growth. Speculation stimulates the concentration of existing wealth. Instead of – indirectly – promoting extended reproduction, it leads to its stagnation and greater exclusion. Falling and even negative economic growth rates and rising exploitation and unemployment rates attest to this limited reproduction, demonstrating that the peak of individual efficiency also negates the Common Good.

Reproduction and the Concept of Vitality

Following the concept of productive and nonproductive labour, we can examine the reproductive logic that will help explain the concept of vitality. Since labour related to social form is considered nonproductive *by-content* in all societies, this applies to both live and materialized labour. Labour materialized in buildings, equipment or materials produced in a particular cycle, and allocated in later cycles to nonproductive spheres such as commerce or finances, is wealth that is consumed nonproductively. It is taken from the production sphere and invested in that of circulation, which is the social relation inherent to that mode of production.

Neoclassical and especially the neoliberal perspectives claim that market relations are natural, absolute and eternal, which leads them to confuse social form and content. Productive labour is that which generates a profit for capital even if it produces no use value or wealth.

According to Altvater and Feerkhuizen: 'In the bourgeois system of production, all labour that preserves or increases its base – capital – can be defined as productive, while labour that is not necessary within this system is seen as nonproductive' (ibid.: 6).

Materialized labour can apparently be classified as productive or nonproductive according to its allocation: it is productive in the reproductive sphere, and nonproductive in that of circulation. This seems arbitrary at first, but not when analysed within a reproductive context. Material goods created in a given cycle of capital include the value and surplus value that is realized only through their sale. Goods created during that cycle increase existing social wealth, while the portion that is nonproductively consumed during the next cycle, as buildings and equipment in the circulation sphere, appears in that second cycle as nonproductively used wealth. This nonproductive investment indirectly may generate economic growth when it leads to better circulation of goods and accelerates subsequent production of surplus value.

Since circulation is functional for production, the spheres appear equally 'productive' to neoclassical economists unconcerned with content. The result is well known and according to Altvater: 'When calculating the national income it is difficult to distinguish between the production of value and its consumption. All revenues are seen as portions of the "big pie", of the social product' (ibid.: 8).

Kozlik reasons that: 'Labour produces value. Allocation of value determines income. Income is only possible because labour creates value that is distributed' (1968: 178). But he goes on to state that: 'Bourgeois consciousness inverts this fact: income produces value. Earning an income proves one has created value for which that is merely compensation.' As a result, according to Kozlik: 'Speculators and brokers are portrayed as useful members of society and worthy of workers' highest regard' (ibid.).

This labour that threatens the system's vitality and negatively affects the conditions for its reproduction as a whole is thus considered by neoclassical economists to be more productive and highly respected than labour that actually contributes to citizens' daily subsistence.

Continuing his analysis of speculation, Kozlik claims that these nonproductive investments detract both directly and indirectly from economic growth. Its negative impact on income distribution results in reduced demand that is not compensated by increased higher incomes since they are also spending more on speculation. This shrinking global demand obstructs productive investment as well as growth:

> Quotation benefits concede the rights to a part of national revenue, regardless of their source. The portion allotted to salaries decreases … These benefits have no effect on real national income … so the use of artificial purchasing power necessarily reduces that of remaining income sectors … When quotations rise more than other prices, shareholders' portion increases while everyone else's decreases … All this, however, does not warrant attention from those who actually compute the national income. (ibid.: 181)

Consumer Society from the Perspective of Efficiency and Vitality

The development of productive forces in capitalism is driven by competition among private interests to maximize profits. This leads to increased constant capital in terms of value on a global social scale. A growing share of value and surplus value is realized in the circulation sphere by owners of the means of production, who are their sole consumers. A increasing mass of means of production is commercialized *in terms of value*, increasing the organic composition of labour, its productivity. Higher labour productivity also means that larger quantities of use values – among other means of consumption – are produced in the same labour period and for the same value. More use values, including means of consumption, must be sold to realize the same amount of value.

The realization of a larger mass of value is conditioned by the sale of a larger mass of means of consumption. This leads to a contradiction, however, since the latter grows more rapidly than the former: 'Two new nonproductive services are developed to overcome this contradiction: advertising and marketing' (Mandel, 1976: 326). To the extent that growing advertising and marketing expenditures indirectly accelerate capital turnaround they are also indirectly productive and thus cost effective, but as that turnaround slows or those expenditures promote the realization of private capital at the expense of others, they are entirely nonproductive (ibid.: 326). 'As the mass of goods increases in relation to the development of productive forces, it becomes more difficult to assess their labour content' (Marx in Mandel, 1976: 326).

But what happens when use value's lifespan decreases? Its physical erosion also leads to a stronger tendency to consume. And what happens to consumer purchasing power? The constant increase in labour productivity decreases the value of goods needed for labour force reproduction, which in turn decreases its own value and raises surplus value rates. The deteriorating lifespan of goods tends to neutralize benefits from the growth of productivity. However, as long as these increases are greater than that rate of deterioration, capital's surplus value rates will continue to rise.

The amount of labour needed to produce goods has decreased with technological development, but declining use value lifespans require it to be duplicated more and more frequently. Wealth produced in the form of value increases at the expense of its durability as use value. Wealth seen by-content that is produced and present in society, and increased by technological development, decreases as a result of the declining lifespan of its use values. For the whole – the citizenry – this means that the same amount of wealth by-content exists but lasts a shorter time. This leads to an irrational wastefulness that obstructs vitality by directing resources away from the satisfaction of real needs.

The reproduction of surplus value based on the sum of private interests and at the expense of material wealth's durability leads to the waste of use values to realize exchange values. From the perspective of an economic rationality grounded in the Common Good or citizens' interest, and not just the general interest of capital, reproduction seen by-content – based on use values – is redirected towards the monetary sphere. This logic is based on realizing exchange values while making an abstraction of use values. It undermines the vitality of the reproduction of wealth by not dealing with new needs or the new poor.

Just as in Adam Smith's times, the concepts of productive and nonproductive labour are again being used in social struggle, this time against a crumbling monopoly capitalism: 'As Bischoff's group pointed out, Baran and Sweezy (1966) moralize by designating all labour that is not necessary in a rationally organized society as nonproductive' (Altvater and Feerkhuizen, 1978: 10). At issue in this discussion is the opposition between an economic rationality based on efficiency and one grounded in Common Good-centred economic regulation.

This rationality based on efficiency enables monopoly capitalism to become more competitive, and to secure more concentrated and geographically broader markets. Technological superiority allows it to produce cheaper, less durable goods and expand its markets across space and time. What is logical for individual capital is not logical for global social capital. As the organic composition of monopoly capital increases in order to control larger market segments, there is a tendency towards increased unused capacity and therefore falling benefit rates in the economy as a whole. This demonstrates once again that the sum of individual-level efficiency does not result in vitality for the whole.

Capitalist development includes a modality that ensures that use values' social lives end even before their technical usefulness is exhausted. In a *consumer-of-value society* the attributes of a product's content are subordinate to its prospects of valuation. Fashion is a wonderful means of shortening the useful life of social use values before their technical utility is depleted. Valuation can be repeated even though existing wealth is still technically present; socially it no longer matters. Thus the subordination of use value to exchange value also includes external variations.

As the consumer-of-value society develops it produces more and more articles whose use value is tied more exclusively to their existence as exchange values – it is increasingly difficult to distinguish utility and content. This is true fetishization of goods: according to the rationality of efficiency, an item's use value can be determined only by the fact that it was sold. Therefore, the exchange value is the only evidence of use value. The rationality of the Common Good asserts that satisfaction of needs and satisfaction of wishes are not interchangeable and could only detract from vitality and the possibility of fulfilling life's basic needs.

This tendency also applies to the consumption of means of production. Competition among capital increases their technical depreciation rates, resulting in shorter social than technical utility and permanent replacement by means of production with such short technical lifespans that it becomes increasingly difficult to recuperate innovation costs. From the perspective of content and of the whole, the growth of productivity resulting from technological development is cancelled by technology's shrinking lifespan. According to the rationality of the Common Good, increased capital turnover ultimately leads to declining production and consumption prospects that are squandered – sacrificed for vitality – on the perpetual realization of value by *private capital in search of efficiency*.

Wastefulness appears to be irrational from the Common Good perspective but is rational from that of efficiency. According to authors such as Kozlik (1968), Mandel (1972) and Aglietta (1979), the economy of waste stems from the contradiction that production's prospects exceed capitalist consumption and investment: 'Those who wish to consume lack sufficient income and those with high incomes do not consume – this fact is a consequence of unequal income distribution. Capital formation exceeds investment possibilities' (Kozlik, 1968: 265). Underutilized factories and machinery are evidence of this excess capital investment: 'Investments exceeding production's requirements create the capacity for overproduction: these are overinvestments of capital. They illustrate that both capital formation and investment have grown more than the possibilities for investment in production' (ibid.: 183).

Waste and increasingly aggressive disputes over the world market are the only ways to avoid overproduction of capital. Waste – irrational reproduction from a Common Good perspective but rational from that of efficiency – assumes many forms under capitalism including: publicity expenses; seduction of consumers into satisfying desires instead of needs; production of goods that wear out quickly; and the production and constant replacement of superfluous equipment, especially arms and aerospace projects (Sweezy, 1970; Mandel, 1976; and Nadal Egea, 1991).

Vitality, Efficiency and Military Expenditure

Defence spending is an important category of nonproductive expenditures that I have previously examined in a book about the Cold War (Dierckxsens, 1994). Here I will focus on this spending in the abstract, relating it to the concepts of vitality and efficiency. Defence and other forms of wasteful spending all involve:

Table 1.1 Military spending and productivity

Country	Military spending (%) of GDP 1985	Average annual growth in productivity of all components 1960–73	1973–80
Japan	1	5.8	3.2
West Germany	3.2	3.6	3.4
France	4.1	4.6	2.8
United Kingdom	5.3	2.6	0.1
United States	6.6	2.4	0.3

Source: Nadal Egea, 1991: 229.

> production of goods whose value is realized in the market but that are not involved in the reproduction process. This leads to increased national revenue (in the primary cycle) accompanied by an absolute decline of existing constant capital funds (in the secondary cycle) and a significant decrease in labour productivity. (Mandel, 1972: I, 311)

This chain illustrating labour's nonproductivity can be extended. The development of machinery in one cycle to produce other machines in a second, to produce defence-related goods in a third, which will disappear from the reproductive sphere in a fourth, demonstrates the nonproductive impact of the military industrial complex in the later stages where much of this spending is channelled. Defence spending operates as though productive forces were not developed to their full potential, in other words at the expense of vitality, as illustrated in Table 1.1. Two basic concerns have fuelled the heated debate over both ethical and economic perspectives on demilitarization during the 1990s:

> the first involves the disappearance of the 'threats' that had generated and justified the arms race. The second is that the military has become a drain on resources, especially for the major powers, and in the long term has eroded their bases of power. (Aguirre and Malgesini, 1991: 29)

The reconversion of military industries to civilian uses has again brought this topic to the forefront. Benoit (1973: 265) claims in this context that its overall effect will be positive: 'Shifts in military spend-

Table 1.2 Comparative profit rates in military and civilian industries (annual averages, 1970–74)

Industry	Pentagon contracts	Commercial activity
Aeroplanes	11.2	6.9
Electronics	15.3	10.0
Missiles	20.0	6.9
Ships	5.8	–
Others	11.5	–
Weighted average	13.5	10.7

Source: Nadal Egea, 1991: 261.

ing have a substantial impact on growth, savings and the balance of trade. If its relative participation in the GDP falls by one percentage point the growth rate will increase by more than one third of one percent.'

West (1991), Deger (1985), and Faini et al. (1984) claim that although defence spending negatively impacts on economic growth, lowering it will require larger investment (West, 1991: 454). Efficiency-led capitalism can see only as far as immediate profits. If they are higher in the defence sector investment will tend to gravitate there regardless of greater or lesser prospects for growth: '[Private] capitalists' goal consists of making a profit, capital accumulation for profit rather than accumulation for the sake of accumulation' (Mandel, 1972: 246).

However, Mandel goes on to state: 'since the expansion of the arms economy assumes the redistribution of surplus value in favor of a handful of companies at the expense of many others, the growth of the military industrial complex will shrink the profits of many companies' (ibid.). Thus it also affects capital's general interests. From general capital's perspective there is clear opposition to the arms race in the civilian economy that seeks to curb its growth. The arms industry from a historical perspective is not of interest here, although it is important to point out some of the causes leading to arms control efforts in the 1990s. In an open economy military spending can be exported to third countries. If the imports a country receives in exchange for arms exports flow into their civilian economy, that nonproductive expenditure will be transferred out at the same rate as its military spending. This illustrates Kozlik's statement (1968: 289) that defence spending is a blessing for advanced capitalist economies – arms producers and exporters. It allows them to follow the efficiency axis of the military industrial complex without sacrificing vitality, and gives them more room for negotiation since they also own the most sophisticated arms.

These same nonproductive expenditures represent a net cost for developing economies – arms importers. They do not provide internal economic benefits or better negotiating positions for dealing with more developed industrialized nations. The Cold War provided an extraordinary climate for such transfers of military spending to third countries.

Defence spending is nonproductive by-content, in other words independent of the social relationships within which it occurs. As a result of proportional spending, the Cold War affected the civilian economy in the Soviet bloc even more than in the West. The end of the Cold War was primarily a result of Soviet initiative and led to disarmament and conversion policies (Melman, 1991: 65). Kozlik (1968: 289) had predicted such a Soviet-initiated end to the arms race in the 1960s. Equivalent military spending was supported by a substantially lower gross domestic product in the USSR, and had a significant impact on its reproductive logic. More than twenty years before the fall of the Berlin Wall Kozlik declared that the USSR:

> is unable to continue to compete and to feed its people and produce needed consumer goods and imports at the same time. It desperately seeks an agreement, but that would also be costly for the West. The Soviet threat becomes even greater when the Russians feel they can redirect military spending to other objectives. (ibid.: 290)

And he concluded that: 'This gives rise to a new justification for arms proliferation ... military spending is advantageous for us, but disadvantageous for the Russians' (ibid.). The discussion clearly focused on a greater loss of vitality for the Soviet compared to the North American economy.

The end of the Cold War also ended the favourable climate for arms sales in the world market and greatly strengthened support for reconversion. Bilateral verification agreements among major powers

Table 1.3 World military spending, 1960–82 (absolute numbers and percentage)

	1960		1970		1975		1980		1982	
	Abs	%	Abs	%	Abs	%	Abs	%	Abs	%
Military spending										
World	345	100	533	100	571	100	645	100	708	100
Industrialized world	321	93	464	89	474	83	533	83	575	81
Third World	24	7	59	11	97	17	112	17	133	19
Arms exports										
World	2.5	100	5.8	100	13.3	100	30.1	100	39.5	100
Industrialized world	2.4	93	5.6	87	12.6	95	28.8	96	35	89
Third World	0.1	4	0.2	3	0.7	5	1.3	4	4.5	11
Arms imports										
World	2.5	100	5.9	100	12.2	100	30.2	100	40	100
Industrialized world	1.4	56	2	34	4.5	37	7.4	25	8.2	21
Third World	1.1	44	3.9	66	7.7	63	22.8	75	31.8	79
*Economic aid**										
World	5.1	100	8.6	100	21.8	100	40.1	100	37.4	100
Industrialized world	5	98	79	92	15.4	71	30	75	31.2	83
Third World	0.1	2	0.7	8	6.4	29	10.1	25	6.2	17

Note: * Delivered
Source: CEPII, 1989: 288–9.

Table 1.4 Military R&D as a percentage of total state-financed R&D expenditure, 1985

Country	Percentage of total public spending on military R&D
Israel	72
United States	70
Soviet Union	60
United Kingdom	30
France	20
Sweden	18
India	17
West Germany	5
Japan	0.8

Source: Nadal Egea, 1991: 251.

in the arms race and the nuclear non-proliferation treaty are evidence of this (Shaw, 1991: 87). However, 'there is a new strategy for world political-military confrontation. Anti-drug, anti-terrorism, anti-nationalism, anti-revolutionary wars ... have replaced the Cold War' (Melman, 1991: 47).

Defence spending has traditionally been justified by claims that cutting-edge innovations from the military industrial complex also fuel the civilian economy, indirectly vitalizing it. Several authors of past and present, including Kozlik and Mandel, have supported this notion, while others, such as Vance, Nadal Egea and Molas Gallart, have argued against it. 'Undoubtedly military spending on scientific research has led to the growth of new technologies and new products' (Kozlik, 1968: 287). Military industrial research and development feeds back into the organic composition of capital in the civilian economy, justifying a substantial portion of government spending on research and development (R&D), especially in the United States (see Table 1.4).

Mandel discusses Vance's proposal that defence spending curbs development of the organic composition of capital in the civilian economy. Vance does not recognize any feedback between these two sectors, but Mandel argues that feedback and thus *spin-offs* are significant (Mandel, 1972: 247).

Nadel Egea (1991) and Molas Gallart (1991) have recently resumed this debate. The latter claims that the growing separation between the military and civilian economies is due to 'the extreme complexity of military programs and their substantial investment needs' (Molas Gallart, 1991: 389). On the other hand, Nadel Egea (1991: 257) argues that: 'Defense-related industries have generally proven to be poor exporters of technology to civilian sectors.'

Enormous investment in the highly technology-intensive missile and aerospace vehicle industries – almost one-third of all US federal R&D funding – resulted in a technological export coefficient of just 3.4%, as measured by patent transfers, while exports to other industries within the same civilian sphere reached almost 50% (ibid.: 254–7). These branches, characterized by highly specialized technology, are becoming more and more disconnected from the civilian economy. It is increasingly difficult to apply technology produced by the aerospace industry to the civilian economy. Feedback between sectors has decreased, highlighting defence spending's purely nonproductive nature.

The Disconnection between Environmental Efficiency and Vitality

The economy of waste in general, and the military industrial complex in particular, endanger the reproduction of natural resources, and in so doing undermine one of the objective conditions for reproduction in general. The relationship between the economy and ecology has been studied more or less systematically since the 1970s by authors such as Taylor (1970), McHarg (1969), Beckerman (1972), Downs (1973), and Pearce (1985). Our interest here lies more specifically in the (dis)connection between environmental efficiency and vitality.

When wealth produced in the form of value – quantifiable resources – increases at the expense of use values' average social life expectancy, the realization of value and surplus value multiplies in time at the expense of resources in the form of increasingly perishable social use values. Given their continuing disappearance, reproduction of social use values must accelerate to meet the same or increasingly fetishized needs, instead of satisfying other less alienated ones or those of the poor. Fetishization of needs transforms them into simple wants, whose existence and satisfaction are subject to efficiency. Satisfaction of needs, generating vitality, is subordinated to the objective conditions of reproduction: human resources, nature, and society as a whole.

The valuation of capital involves a dual spiral of waste. Permanent accumulation through increasingly aggressive realization of value leads to a growing assault on nature (see Gutman, 1986; Morin, 1980; Bifani, 1980; and Schmidt, 1976, among others). 'The rationality of capitalist natural resource exploitation ... that seeks to maximize private profit in the short term, results in a decline of tropical ecosystems' productive capacity' (Leff, 1986: 47).

For capital, nature is an external factor of the economy. 'For capital nature becomes an object to be subordinated and is no longer seen as a force in and of itself' (Quaini, 1977: 123). Natural wealth reproduces on its own or can be substituted within its niche. As such it has no value and is not included in a monetary economy's bookkeeping – it is not considered wealth. Consequently, by allowing more frequent valuation this waste is actually, and irrationally, thought to increase rather than exhaust wealth.

From an efficiency perspective, it is ironic that as more wealth is squandered in the valuation of capital, there is more development, and more measurable wealth is produced. On the other hand, declining use value lifespans also entail their return to the natural environment as waste matter. With this loss of value comes the loss of their real mission in a monetary economy and they are discarded as waste, polluting nature and degrading the environment. There is development according to the rationality of efficiency. But from the rationality of the Common Good, could there be any greater loss of production wealth than this?

Does capitalism have internal mechanisms of its own to avoid the increasing destruction of nature and degradation of the environment? Consider this question from a global perspective. At the dawn of capitalism, when nature was relatively abundant for the needs of capital reproduction, its exploitation was extensive. After becoming relatively exhausted in some countries, for example, in Europe, its exploitation was increasingly extended to peripheral countries. Nature and natural reproduction have played a significant role in worldwide extended reproduction of capital:

Capital, in its global expansion, appropriated resources from the

> planet's diverse ecosystems. During the first two centuries of capitalist accumulation the relative abundance of natural resources hindered research on their conservation and reproduction. (Leff, 1986: 34)

However, this extended reproduction, especially since its monopolistic phase, does not just extend across space, but as previously shown, also intensifies in time, leading to more intensive exploitation of natural resources and greater environmental pollution.

> In this way, the extended reproduction of capital caused accelerated exploitation of limited natural and biotic resources whose regeneration requires slower use than that imposed by capital reproduction. The resulting increased resource depletion has led to higher prices for raw materials and for goods in general … all of which obstructs the re-elevation of surplus value rates and profit rates. (ibid.: 39)

An imbalance between these two reproduction processes occurs as the regeneration of finite natural and biotic resources becomes slower than that imposed by the extended reproduction of capital. Capital reproduction is a process of valuation that can survive only as long as there is content, and as it disappears the process is obstructed. Imbalances between environmental and capital reproduction result in the growing need to conserve nature as substitutions and other alternatives are depleted:

> The innovation of new 'environmental' technologies that allow more rational exploitation of different ecosystems – from the perspective of natural resource reproduction – has become the necessary condition for capital's survival … These technological resources are, however, insufficient to overcome the effects of capitalist accumulation on ecological destruction. (ibid.: 40)

The natural conditions of production gradually turn against the rationality of capital, giving rise to increasingly intense ecological debate. This debate and the ensuing environmental policy unfold in a climate where the real solution to the environmental crisis is gradually exacerbated, before providing the solution:

> Environmental policies have had the task of restoring market rationality by expanding it to include the natural environment. Neoclassical economics offers a theoretical explanation for it: a new market is

> created as the natural environment is appraised and the costs incurred by functional losses are calculated. (Verhagen, 1978: 18)

As a result, the main problem is merely the availability of data needed to calculate those costs:

> Paradoxically, environmental policies have allowed the very capital that generated the environmental crisis to benefit from it as well. These policies generate a lucrative new industry – eco-industry – in two ways: the State generates a market for measuring instruments ... and the State creates a market for environmental clean-up technologies. (ibid.)

After environmental expenses have been calculated and the degree of contamination has been measured according to the rationality of efficiency, the next step involves purchasing the rights to the contamination, to natural resource waste, etc., instead of resolving the underlying problem. Environmental costs are included among general production costs. Consequently, 'environmental experts have recognized that the market economy has triggered the ecological crisis, but that those same market principles applied to the environment can lead to its solution' (Krusewitz, 1978: 82).

Critical authors such as Taylor (1970) and Leff (1986) analyse instead neoclassical economics' limitations by reducing the ecological crisis to market economics:

> Because of the difficulties involved in evaluating and operationalizing these ecological processes ... in economic calculations and concrete planning activities, environmental management of development, in the broadest sense, has been limited to ... a political economy of pollution. (Leff, 1986: 138)

Contrasting the market's economic rationality with a Common Good and vitality-centred logic, Leff concludes:

> The pollution economy evaluates environmental deterioration as equivalent to the amount of resources that must be used to return it to its natural state. However ... no amount of investment can regenerate ecosystems that have been transformed or degraded beyond a certain point. (ibid.: 143)

He goes on to state:

> The rehabilitation costs of the ecodestruction generated by the market-driven economic rationality is minor compared to the productive potential of integral resource management that follows a rationality ... based on other objectives and values. (ibid.: 143)

Leff is referring here to a Common Good-centred rationality. It has been clear for several decades that, regarding natural resource reproduction, the Common Good must be defined in global terms. However, inasmuch as the market economy promotes private sector efficiency, it is difficult to find a true commitment to the whole where ecological issues are concerned.

> Serious interest in resource conservation requires recognition first and foremost that this is a global issue ... It is of little or no interest that one or several countries opt for resource conservation policies if others continue with wasteful ones. (Closkey, 1988: 136)

Conscious of actors outside of national controls, the author refines his argument pointing out that:

> a global approach is also necessary since serious conservation policies require that multinational businesses ... be controlled and held responsible to the world community of nations. (ibid.: 136)

Politics and ethics scholars' concern for the Common Good and ecology is related to conservation of vegetable or animal species and virgin lands. But not all interest in conservation is centred on the Common Good. Preservation as an end in and of itself and its resulting conservationism is politically intolerant. These conservationists conclude that if there is not room for all species then the human species should be the one to yield:

> Politically intolerant conservationism requires the State to act with intolerance, imposing its own preferences and value judgements on the community in general, even though such actions may go against the well-being of the community, even of the world community. (ibid.: 129)

Destructive *laissez faire* policies must be changed in order to conserve natural resources (Kraft, 1977: 186). Substituting free market competition with a centralized conservationist plan risks totalitarian conservationist solutions. In this context Closkey proposes ecological regulation linked to economic regulation:

> Much can be achieved by reducing waste without lowering standards of living or of enjoyment … Advocates of the no-growth doctrine show incredible insensitivity toward the needs and rights of nations and their inhabitants … Instead of incentives for wastefulness, incentives against waste could be introduced. (Closkey, 1988: 145)

These regulations' horizons should be squarely based on the Common Good. In this context the author concludes: 'The only open and realistic path toward political reform is through political institutions in an open society respectful of human rights' (ibid.: 170).

2

Globalization and the Casino Economy

The So-called Class War

Two major periods since the Second World War have led up to the current financial crisis. The first is characterized by strong productive investment and sustained growth clearly fostered by state intervention. The result was greater social involvement, often in a social contract that granted negotiated participation to the working class. In the second period, beginning in the late 1960s and early 1970s, investments gradually abandoned the productive sphere and became more transnational. This trend is evident in the expansion of financial capital throughout the world. The social welfare state was also dismantled during this time, resulting in greater exclusion of the working class and the loss of its negotiated participation.

The first period led to extended reproduction of productive capital (formation of fixed assets), along with stimulated labour productivity and economic growth (see Tables 2.1a and 2.1b). As productive investment decreased in the second period, capital became less productive (see Table 2.2), as it gambled instead on the prospect of greater future exploitation. The productive sphere was abandoned as the mechanisms were reinforced for redistribution and concentration of existing wealth. During the past 20 years considerable effort has gone into achieving those much-anticipated prospects, but without success. Now we must try to avoid a repetition of 1929, not so much for humanitarian reasons, but because such extensive destruction of fictitious capital would shake capitalism's very foundations (Bonefeld and Holloway, 1995: 23).

The crisis of capitalist reproduction originated in its flight from

Table 2.1a Growth rates: population, GDP and labour productivity, 1913–89 (change in average annual compound growth rates)

	Increase from 1913–50 to 1950–73 per capita				Decrease from 1950–73 to 1973–89 per capita			
	Population	GDP	GDP	Labour productivity	Population	GDP	GDP	Labour productivity
Australia	0.8	2.5	1.7	1.2	-0.8	-1.6	-0.7	-0.9
Austria	0.3	5.1	4.7	5.0	-0.4	-2.9	-2.5	-2.2
Belgium	0.2	3.1	2.8	3.0	-0.4	-2.0	-1.5	-1.4
Canada	0.5	2.0	1.4	0.5	-1.0	-1.5	-0.4	-1.1
Denmark	-0.4	1.3	1.6	2.5	-0.6	-2.1	-1.5	-2.5
Finland	-0.1	2.2	2.4	2.9	-0.3	-1.8	-1.6	-3.0
France	0.9	3.9	2.9	3.1	-0.5	-2.7	-2.2	-1.8
Germany	1.7	4.6	4.2	4.9	-0.9	-3.8	-2.9	-3.3
Italy	0.0	4.1	4.2	3.8	-0.4	-2.7	-2.4	-3.2
Japan	-0.1	7.1	7.1	5.8	-0.4	-5.4	-4.9	-4.5
Netherlands	-0.1	2.3	2.3	3.5	-0.6	-2.7	-2.0	-2.4
Norway	0.0	1.2	1.1	1.7	-0.4	-0.1	0.4	-0.7
Sweden	0.0	1.3	1.2	1.6	-0.4	-2.0	-1.5	-2.8
Switzerland	0.9	1.9	1.0	0.6	-1.2	-3.2	-2.1	-2.1
United Kingdom	0.2	1.7	1.7	1.6	-0.4	-1.0	-0.7	-0.9
United States	0.2	1.2	0.6	0.1	-0.4	-0.9	-0.6	-1.5
Average	0.3	2.8	2.6	2.6	-0.6	-2.3	-1.7	-2.1

Source: Maddison, 1991: 129.

Table 2.1b OECD: growth rates of various indicators, 1953–95 (average annual variations, percentages)

	53–60	60–65	65–73	73–79	79–85	85–89	89–95	50–73	73–95
GDP	2.9	5.3	5.0	2.7	2.1	3.4	1.8	4.3	2.4
Private consumption	2.9	5.1	5.1	3.0	2.1	3.5	2.0	4.3	2.6
Fixed asset formation	4.4	7.1	5.9	1.2	1.1	5.3	1.8	5.7	2.1
Consumer prices	2.5	2.6	4.8	10.3	7.5	3.5	3.4	3.4	6.4

Source: Shutt, 1998: 38.

Table 2.2 Growth of productivity of capital, 1913–84 (average annual growth rates)

	1913–50	1950–73	1973–84	1913–84
Germany	0.56	0.57	-1.71	0.20
United States	0.96	0.34	-0.47	0.55
France	0.12	1.50	-1.82	0.23
Japan	0.69	1.39	-3.41	0.28
Netherlands	0.31	0.85	-1.83	0.15
United Kingdom	0.13	-0.26	-1.45	-0.24
Average	0.46	0.73	-1.78	0.20

Source: Maddison, 1996: 49.

productive labour. Accumulation is based on the concentration of existing wealth and gambling on future prospects rather than the real valuation of capital. The monetary crisis and destruction of fictitious capital on a global scale, provide evidence that the wager has been lost. As Bonefeld and Holloway have stated (1995: 11), the crisis of capital is essentially the crisis of its dependency on productive labour.

Since the late 1970s, falling profit rates have plagued productive labour's involvement. In that decade, capital began to abandon the productive sphere, taking refuge in the fantastic world of self-expanding money, gambling on future prospects for including the labour force at higher profit rates. This wager involves capital's hope to use labour more profitably at a later time. In other words, the insubordination of productive labour has led capital to abandon productive branches for the financial sphere (ibid.). The hope is to face this challenge by operating outside the productive sphere to obtain greater benefits from production itself. Thurow (1996: 180) refers to this as a declaration of 'class war from above'.

Monetarism, which is the decree of purely monetary accumulation, is essentially the accumulation of 'unemployed capital' that no longer uses (productive) labour, gambling instead on more intensive exploitation in the future. Capital accumulates monetary wealth without a corresponding use of labour in the productive sphere, and seeks to realize profits through greater concentration of existing wealth.

High monetary profits can easily be obtained and are unlimited by

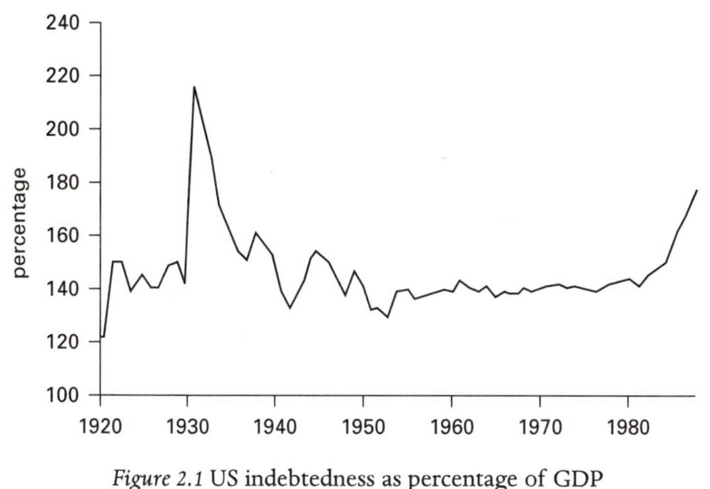

Figure 2.1 US indebtedness as percentage of GDP
(*Source*: Chevallier, 1998: 103)

boundaries in the financial sphere. In this process of globalization capital feels liberated from the discomforts of productive labour and boundary restrictions. The retreat to the 'rational' accumulation of capital merely indicates an effort to increase profit rates through greater exploitation of labour in the productive sphere. The monetarist project consists of using money to neutralize the power of productive labour. The shift away from productive labour actually leads to increased exploitation and flexibility of the remaining productive labour. Bonefeld and Holloway (ibid.) conclude that if productive labour is not used more efficiently, the stimulating prospects of the money supply for more intensive future exploitation will lead to massive capital devaluation.

The desperation surrounding this gamble is apparent in the intense and prolonged efforts to use productive labour for greater worldwide benefits. Despite all the misery and poverty caused by abandoning productive labour, that is, despite exclusion, capital reproduction through a return to the productive sphere has been unsuccessful. It turns instead to the expansion of credit without previous savings (debts) to finance its gamble on the more profitable future use of labour in the productive sphere (see Figure 2.1).

Unlimited expansion of credit leads to increasing private debt:

The relentless rise of financial markets involves an insuppressible

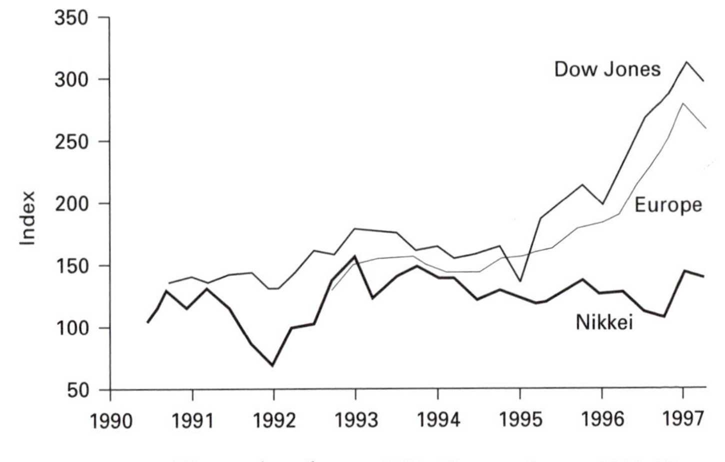

Figure 2.2 The stock exchange: USA, Europe, Japan, 1990–97
(*Source*: Chevallier, 1998: 183)

> appetite for debt ... It is not surprising that debt increased exponentially both in the 1920s and in the 1980s ... The crisis of wealthy nations' banking systems in the late 1980s has revealed that excessive Third World debt is minor compared to that of industrialized nations ... Shareholders' short-term satisfaction has become the primary goal ... The uninterrupted climb of financial markets since 1982 can be interpreted as a new form of inflation. (Chevallier, 1988: 99–103)

This inflation is not in the price of goods as in the 1960s, but in stock prices as illustrated in Figure 2.2.

Thus, in the last instance, increasingly there is as yet unproduced surplus value being committed. We can speak of a casino economy when capital accumulation depends on this gamble as well as on rising credit unsupported by necessary savings. The state must guarantee that credit to avoid an eventual collapse. Greater cuts in government social spending – for housing, health care and social security – along with greater austerity and reduction of internal debt will leave more room to meet the private gamble on future prospects. Everything working for the Common Good must be sacrificed to safeguard these prospects.

The more the general existence of capital is based on credit that is unsupported by savings, the greater the need to change labour practices and technology and to increase the benefits obtained from labour.

It is not possible to support credit indefinitely. Capital must achieve higher benefits by its future use of productive labour. The inability to do this is revealed by the continued expansion of credit to cover this gamble on future prospects. As yet there has been no real shift towards expanding productive investment. Only 5% of the shares traded in the market are new offerings; the remaining 95% represent acquisitions, mergers, and the like. The gamble on future prospects is perpetuated. This leads to a rapid increase of stocks traded on the market, that is, supported by a growing inverted pyramid of credit. This unbridled gamble is evidence of the inability to make more beneficial use of productive labour.

Continuation of this crisis and its possible outcome are not merely threats. They also are a message of hope – that capital flight from productive labour will lead to massive destruction of fictitious capital and the objective need to regulate a return to productive labour. Money as credit can lead to what Thurow has called 'class war from above'. However, when credit is unable to return to the productive sphere, it becomes a weapon that is aimed at the destruction of capital itself (Bonefeld and Holloway, 1995: 8, 20–2).

The Connection Between Money and Productive Labour

To grasp the connection between money and productive labour, it is necessary to understand that production and circulation processes jointly include the possibility of crisis and confrontation. Their interrelationship is established through money but becomes less transparent when credit is involved. Credit predominates throughout the world today and is the best weapon for more flexibility in labour and for more intensively exploiting it. Neither money nor credit is outside of reproduction, although credit temporarily allows reproduction of profits but not the reproduction of productive capital.

As a general equivalent, money is the material representation of wealth in general; that is, of labour in general. The social nature of all individual labour becomes evident in exchanges that are mediated by money. As a general equivalent, it is the universal form assumed by labour in the market economy; in circulation it need not appear in the form of material goods. As commerce developed faster than the production of gold, metallic currency was replaced by paper money that could be converted to gold. Since those who hold paper money do not usually try to convert their bills into gold at the same time, gold reserves need not cover all the paper money in circulation. Bank notes are 'as good as gold' so long as the central banks guarantee their convertibility.

Indirect convertibility of paper money to gold occurs when the convertibility of one currency is expressed in terms of another, and one of them is expressed in terms of gold (as with the US dollar). In 1970, 60% of international reserves were held in foreign exchange and 40% in gold. By 1980 more than 80% of reserves were held in foreign exchange (Paz, 1983: 134–9). In the early 1970s the automatic convertibility of the US dollar to gold was terminated. As a result the relationship between the value of goods and of gold is not an instant given. The value of paper money can be expressed only by free (black) market exchange rates or by the price of gold expressed in that currency. Only then does the concept of inflation begin to emerge (Mandel, 1972: 337).

Money as potential capital and as an instrument for producing profits originates not from an act of buying and selling but in the movement of capital. Both lender and borrower invest the same amount of money – the first as owner and the second as user – so that the borrower can use it as capital. It can only work as capital for both when they divide between them the profit it produces. The lender's share of the profit is called interest. Since interest is a part of the profit it cannot exceed the profit, even though interest rates can vary with relative independence according to the supply and demand of money capital (Marx, 1973: III, 364–76).

To accumulate money and make it available for production is to constitute and then lend monetary capital. This act of lending can be distinguished from credit that actually creates money. A loan is the use of monetary capital previously accumulated and stored to create greater future wealth. Credit, on the other hand, is assigned based on the ownership of future commodities produced by future labour. Bankers lend more than they have amassed, thus creating debts to themselves, while industrialists make use of payments promised to productive capital by injecting them into the productive economy to gain surplus value. When productive capital succeeds at using labour for sufficient benefit in the future, the gamble pays off. If not, the industrialists and the bankers both lose and risk ruin.

Expanding credit based on debts rather than on previous savings results in the creation of money. Bank credit frees projected investments from the restrictions that are imposed by currently available savings. This involves a gamble on labour and savings that must be mobilized in the future. To allow certain agents to gamble more than their actual earnings, policies must be introduced requiring others – the state and salaried workers – to spend less with the hope of increasing productive capacity (CEPII, 1996: 194). This austerity imposed on society as a whole for the benefit of speculative capital strangles the real economy, which is the productive economy (Shutt, 1998: 47).

By lowering benefit rates in the West since the 1970s, capital over the past 25 years has gambled more and more on the future exploitation of labour. The expansion of credit based on private debt that has backed this gamble has not led to a corresponding expansion of productive labour for capital; in fact, it has strangled the real (productive) economy (Shutt, 1998: 47, 55). The gamble on future prospects actually leads much capital to insolvency and in the long term to bankruptcy. Nonproductive use of capital that does not become more productive leads to the general devaluation of social capital. The nonconvertibility of nonproductive capital will dramatically demystify the fictitious dimension of capital's control over labour (Bonefeld, 1995: 84). Credit grows much faster than money tied to real wealth. The unlimited credit offered to the latter cases was based on the belief that these investments would become productive in the short term without anticipating market-imposed limitations.

The fictitious and speculative nature of credit-based accumulation comes to light when the pseudovalidation of surplus value is tied to the accumulation of stocks or rights over future labour. Their value is real to the extent that the nominal increase of shares will result in an expansion of the reproductive process. As negotiable paper, however, their nominal value can increase or decrease in the stock market independent of the real capital that their owners control. The shares' market value is not determined by the firm's real revenue but by its anticipated future earnings, which, therefore, is speculation (Marx, 1973: III, 470, 480).

As long as an inverted pyramid of credit supports the speculative phase, the gamble is 'freed' from productive labour, which is the real economy and will be able to strongly confront it. By investing in the speculative sphere capital can operate relatively poor without productive labour, resulting in more flexible involvement and greater benefit rates. But there are limits to this withdrawal. The market tends to contract along with the possibilities in the real economy to make a profit. Fictitious capital will collapse the day that expectations of real profit-making disappear along with the possibility of prolonging the virtual economy. Capital itself will incur tremendous losses.

Privatization of Global Financial Management

The world market is the most developed mode of integrating abstract labour and the form of value. The expansion of abstract wealth based on global productive labour is slower than the expansion of money's power when not linked to that labour. This explains why globalization results from the gamble on future exploitation without any real capacity to create such productive 'employment'. Economic regulation vanishes in this process and money's power is privatized throughout the world and at the expense of labour.

The development of credit contracts for any nation can be expressed as a chain of promissory notes in which money figures only abstractly in the accounts. Nevertheless, when the credits and debts are not compensated, the remaining promissory notes must be settled with a true commodity – money. This requires there be real value reserve funds that are the foundation of a nation's monetary stability.

National reserves guarantee the existence of credit in terms of a currency's convertibility to real wealth and so determine the limits of sustained accumulation. The flight of reserves from any given nation-state is expressed as a negative balance of payments. It represents a potential threat to the currency's convertibility to commodities in the world market (Bonefeld, 1995: 87–9). International credit guarantees and the very stability of the entire international financial system depend on the relationship between the amount of credit granted and the existing international reserves. These guarantees, which are regulated by the 1944 Bretton Woods Accord, do not currently exist.

The Bretton Woods Accord established the gold standard: that monetary reserves would include US dollars, and secondarily, British pounds. The agreement laid the foundation for global bookkeeping by linking currencies to the US dollar and the dollar, in turn, to gold. This was needed to prevent circulation from abandoning production and becoming increasingly speculative. Until the mid-1960s central bank authorities from the Group of Ten and international financial agencies were able to use these Accords to neutralize speculative pressures (Paz, 1983: 156–8).

The expansion of private banking through credit outside of official controls began in the late 1960s. This growth had been very limited throughout the 1950s and early 1960s as until then the official agencies, both multilateral and bilateral, were the primary source of international loans and credit. In 1965 international private banking began to operate in the international market with a significant expansion of uncontrolled credit (ibid.) rooted in burgeoning productive direct foreign investment throughout the world.

The resulting tide of private investment surpasses borders and is independent of official controls. In 1964, such private international credits represented less than 20% of international reserves, an amount still easily controlled by the central banks. Rapid changes in management and control were required as their growth significantly increased in succeeding years. By 1970, these credits were 70% of total international reserves (ibid.: 156–8). The result was an ever more inverted pyramid: unbridled development of international credit that was backed by diminishing reserves of foreign exchange (paper money) and even less of gold. It is in this context that international banking credit for Latin America was developed, resulting in the foreign debt crisis of the 1980s.

Monetary authorities controlled private international credit and speculation, though with increasing difficulty. There was mounting pressure from speculation. The monetary instability that began in 1968 culminated in 1971 with the termination of the US dollar's convertibility to gold. That year more than 60% of international reserves were held in foreign exchange and 40% in gold; by 1980 more than 80% were in foreign exchange (ibid.: 134–9). After 1971, certain economies enjoyed a strong positive balance of trade. The mark and yen were gradually able to challenge the US dollar in international reserves. In 1977 these holdings represented 20% of all foreign exchange reserves, and almost 40% by 1993 (OECD, 1995: 17). However, the US dollar continues to be the world's major currency and the consummate speculative currency.

The breakdown of the Bretton Woods Accord system marked the actual collapse of private banking's regulations against the speculation of private capital. The global development of private credit explains the worldwide monetary crisis that heralded the central banks' fall from power and coincided with the general decline of benefit rates. Conditions were right for the uncontrolled global creation of private bank money outside the channels and rules of monetary institutionality.

Sources and mechanisms increasing the worldwide supply of private bank credit have since diversified and multiplied without central bank control. In 1975, international credits exceeded reserves; by 1980 they were more than double those reserves. During the 1990s, speculators have had unlimited reserves compared to those of official international organizations (Martin and Schumann, 1996: 107). Floating exchange parity was officially agreed upon in 1976 and the IMF was empowered to oversee the exchange policies. None of these measures has worked in practice. Monetary parity has been increasingly volatile, unstable and subject to private speculation (Cleaver, 1995: 45–7).

With the loss of monetary controls over private capital, private banking no longer has exclusive control over the international movement of capital. Large multinational corporations and institutional funds (such as insurance funds and pension plans) now manage international financial capital that is increasingly separate from the real economy. In the mid-1990s, the financial economy as a whole managed 50 times more money than the real economy (Ramonet, 1997a: 1). Between 1970 and 1990, the amount of interbank debt held by private international banks grew twelvefold, and transnational bank credits to non-bank receivers increased 32 times. This tendency intensified in the 1990s (Andreff, 1995: 71).

International reserves seem ridiculously low compared to the strength of private money. Displacement of even 1 or 2% of private finances could now change the parity between two national currencies. Monetary authorities of many countries are unable to defend their exchange rates from the free play of the market and speculation. National economic policies lack autonomy, being subordinate to transnational interests. The international monetary system has become private, speculative and unstable (Andreff, 1995: 71–5).

This private monetary system is the relative domain of the US dollar. Globalization controlled by financial and speculative capital results in the dollarizing of these wagers. More than half of all international foreign exchange reserves – and one-half of the world's savings – are held in US dollars. Speculation is easier using the US currency. The climax of the US dollar in the years just before 1999 was largely the result of speculative investment in that currency.

By controlling the world's largest public and private reserves, the US dollar has also been dominant in international relations. This was a powerful influence in the creation of the European Monetary Union. The new Euro currency seemingly restores official power for better regulation of the financial market. Instead, it is essentially the result of confrontation between private capital of one bloc and that of another, breaking the US dollar's relative dominance (Martin and Schumann, 1996: 105–14; Bonefeld, 1995: 91).

The Divorce Between the Real and the Virtual Economies

Expansion of credit has not been the result of political error. It is a means for capital to elude labour's insubordination that has been disguised as an economic problem. There was a clear example of political insubordination early in the twentieth century. Historically, the 1917 October Revolution in Russia was the first attempt to create an alternative to the capitalist system. Capital then began to retreat from productive sectors in industrialized countries, followed by an expansion of credit in the 1920s and finally to the crash of 1929 (Bonefeld and Holloway, 1995: 8–9). 'The expansion of credit preceding the crash was the other face of the October Revolution's open insubordination, a gamble on future insubordination' (ibid.: 9).

Unable to guarantee greater benefits from the use of productive labour during this period, capital retreated towards nonproductive sectors. For example, there was the tripling of bank credit to finance stock purchases and sales in the USA between January 1927 and October 1929. The Dow Jones Index doubled in just two years, rising by 50% in the first eight months of 1929 (Aglietta, 1979: 317). Current circumstances reveal a similar situation. The Dow Jones Index again doubled in the two years beginning June 1995, reaching a historic high of 8,000 on July 9, 1997 and even higher in April 1999 to 11,000, almost three times 1995 levels in less than four years. Chevallier (1998: 93) has analysed the parallels between the 1920s crisis and our current situation (see Table 2.3).

The actual event triggering the financial crisis is unimportant in such circumstances. The psychological impact of Russia's financial crisis in the summer of 1998 provoked financial panic. Demands for liquidity (cash flow) undermined the scaffold of debt. If business euphoria is the initial manifestation of the virtual accumulation of capital, then financial panic is the initial manifestation of massive capital devaluation. All creditors immediately try to collect on debts, which leads to a chain reaction of general bank and financial insolvency. This explains how the Asian crisis began in Thailand and Malaysia, then, starting in August 1997, spread panic throughout the region. It was clear that financial crisis might spread throughout the world by the Russian crisis. In an eventual run on the market only part of total debt can actually be collected. Stock prices plummet, leading to the ruin of many speculators.

In 1929 the Dow Jones average fell 40% in three weeks, from 327 to 199. More than half of the financial investment companies disappeared within a few weeks. Savings accounts lost 90% of their nominal value. Gross profit rates fell from 12.8% in 1929 to 7.2%, 3.5%, and 1.3% in the following years (Aglietta, 1979: 319–21). Liquid cash flow was resumed only after achieving a level of activity that was compatible with the real value of capital stocks at their new depressed prices.

The 1930s crisis demonstrated that even the largest companies could lose. Similar symptoms are apparent in the current crisis. This revelation of the Common Bad, when even big capital could lose, brought an end to the economic war and the beginning of new Keynesian economic regulation. This transaction was not without worldwide upheaval. Keynes provided an important theoretical foundation for the acceptance of credit controlled by an interventionist state to guarantee more or less strong ties between money and productive labour. Controlled expansion of credit would re-establish the link with productive labour, and thus guarantee full employment with the stable

Table 2.3 The Dow Jones Index, 1912–30 and 1971–89 compared

Year	Min	Max	Year	Min	Max	Year	Min	Max	Year	Min	Max
1930	158	294	1920	67	110	1989	1,580	2,940	1979	797	898
1929	199	381	1919	79	130	1988	1,990	3,810	1978	742	908
1928	191	300	1918	74	89	1987	1,910	3,000	1977	801	1,000
1927	153	202	1917	66	99	1986	1,530	2,020	1976	859	1,015
1926	135	167	1916	85	110	1985	1,185	1,553	1975	632	882
1925	115	159	1915	54	99	1984	1,087	1,287	1974	878	892
1924	88	121	1914	71	83	1983	1,027	1,267	1973	788	1,052
1923	86	105	1913	72	89	1982	777	1,071	1972	889	1,036
1922	79	103	1912	80	94	1981	824	1,024	1971	798	951
1921	64	82				1980	759	1,000			

Source: Chevallier, 1998: 93.

realization of surplus value in circulation. It is an era of controlled, permanent inflation. Central bank controls provided in the Bretton Woods Accords were meant to prevent greater separation between money and production (uncontrolled inflation). This agreement made good bookkeeping, making possible good international controls.

The first decades after the Second World War were characterized by the strong expansion of productive capital. The development of productive forces led to realizing more value and surplus value in the circulation sphere by the owners of the means of production who were their sole consumers. In terms of value, a growing mass of the means of production was commercialized, increasing the organic composition of labour, that is, its productivity.

Higher labour productivity means that larger masses of use values are produced in the same labour period. More use values must be sold to realize the same amount of value. Realization of the means of production's greater social value is conditioned by that of a larger mass of use values with declining social value. This disparity lowers profits, thus increasing the costs of realization.

Increasing physical or cultural erosion in the 1960s intensified the so-called propensity towards consumption (the consumer society and the wasteful society), offsetting the reduction of labour necessary for increased productivity. Capital's surplus value rates increase to the extent that greater productivity exceeds the decrease in the life expectancies of commodities. Realizing this is more difficult, since the payment abilities of consumers are limited. Expansion of consumer credit is an alternative in situations where incomes increase less rapidly than does production. Such credit policies postpone the contradiction without resolving it. This contradiction of underconsumption was the major cause of the 1930s crisis.

The crisis of late capitalism is rooted in the overproduction of the means of production. Competition between larger and larger capital increases the rate of technical depreciation of the means of production, thus gambling on the possibility of greater exploitation in a future cycle. Everyone intends to secure a bigger piece of the pie. This results in shorter socially useful lifespans for installed capacity. Credit develops more rapidly in the sector producing the means of production, given big capital's expectation to have a larger slice of the future pie. On an individual basis, capital made the right bet. On the level of social capital, however, the result was an increase in unused capacity. There is a potential increase in the use of productive labour with greater profit rates, but this does not actually happen.

For Keynes state intervention was necessary to oversee credit and thus to control the relationship between production and money. However, he left resource distribution – credit among sectors – to the free play of the market. This objectively resulted in the development of credit for the means of production, which decreased the use of installed capacity. In late capitalism, free designation of credit results in a tendency to gamble disproportionately on the future exploitation of labour. This leads to the overproduction of constant capital with chronic unused capacity, and erodes the (potential) increase of productivity. Debt grows faster than labour productivity, leading to an upward spiral of permanent inflation (Aglietta, 1979: 328).

Since the 1970s the crisis of late capitalism has been apparent in the inability of monetary capital to keep in step with the reduction of necessary labour requirements. Capital turns to the accumulation of monetary wealth, given decreasing profit rates and thus investment in the productive sphere. Discontinuing the use of credit to control labour effectively by way of 'unemployed' capital, however, is fictitious. Eventually, 'unemployed' capital must be transformed into employed capital to avoid a general devaluation of capital. 'Unemployed' capital can become productive only by making better use of labour in the productive sphere. The stability of money divorced from productive accumulation is feasible only as long as there are expectations of greater future profits. Financial panic tends to break out the moment such expectations are lost.

Both monetarism and Keynesianism are political expressions of the unity, in separation, of production and circulation. Keynesianism supports this unity by favouring demand that results in overproduction of the means of production through credit. Such policies result in inflationary pressures that subordinate the primitive form of monetary capital. Monetarism attacks inflation seeking to amend the split between production and circulation. Vitality of the system is subordinated to immediate profits from the circulation sphere. This is a gamble on the more beneficial future use of productive labour.

Prospects for a Return to Productive Labour

The only way 'unemployed capital' can hope to become employed is through an increase in the profit rate of productive labour. Not being convertible to employed capital intensifies the fictitious dimension of the capitalist control over labour. Only while there is hope of higher future profits is it feasible to separate the stability of money from productive accumulation. The more capital accumulation gambles on future prospects, the more capital will try to maintain the viability of accumulation by reducing labour costs, cutting social spending, and intensifying the labour process.

In an economy where investment is increasingly nonproductive, the growth of the national product stagnates and the gamble on greater future exploitation is overstated, as is the need to maintain promising future scenarios. As long as this perspective continues, credit will finance an upward spiral of speculation and increasing paper profits. This optimism will cause growing unemployment and misery: in other words, at the expense of the decisive defeat of the working class.

The capital–labour conflict intensifies in the casino economy, resulting in a new international division of labour that increasingly excludes productive labour. Although each region starts from a different level of labour stability, the tendency in recent decades has been towards greater flexibility of labour. This has more vertical controls, with a clear loss of the workers' direct involvement in the social orientation and income distribution (Lipietz, 1995: 11).

This trend can be classified as neoTaylorism, and affects the old industrial powers such as the United States and Great Britain. Capitalists in these countries opposed workers having direct negotiated participation as they abandoned Fordism throughout industry. The capitalists were successful and have become even more neoTaylorist (Thurow, 1996: 180). This model breaks down, however, in branches and jobs that require skilled workers and do not have a high level of routine. Participation is essential to labour's productivity. The USA has lost its competitive edge in more than one of these sectors because its workers lacked participation.

Neoliberals have strongly criticized 'euro-sclerosis', attributed to the greater difficulties of the Old World in replacing the labour force and thus having more rigid salary relations. These difficulties are objectively rooted in the generalization of wage relations that have been negotiated in many nations, notably in northern Europe. This social democratic model includes trade unions and employers' associations that negotiate the social orientation and income distribution at regional and national levels.

Increased bets on future prospects have made this model for achieving these adjustments more difficult. More intensive exploitation was obviously resisted by national labour organizations as it leads to more unequal income redistribution that favours capital. Social democratic models have tended to lose their competitive edge in a variety of sectors that are characterized by jobs classified as more routine and less skilled. Workers' collective involvement – with a sense of common destiny shared by businesses and workers in the less routine and more skilled occupations or sectors – can provide a competitive edge over flexibility, but not in the more routine and less-skilled job sectors.

Between 1930 and 1970, industrialization based on import substitution and inspired by peripheral Fordism was developed in Latin America and other peripheral countries. The characteristic form of accumulation featured compromise between state leadership and a 'labour aristocracy'. This model was possible where it was relatively difficult to replace labour, in other words, where wage labour had been developed. This is a somewhat rigid type of Fordism, characterized by involvement of the company and the sector, and, above all, that includes state employees. Recent 'integration' of these countries to the new international division of labour has gradually led to a destruction of import-substitution industrialization to another based on maquilas and the application of primitive neoTaylorism through crude flexibility of labour (Lipietz, 1995: 17).

Eastern nations, such as Japan and the Asian 'Tigers', are examples of dual societies that combine involvement and flexibility. There is participation by successful companies or sectors with high technological development, highly skilled labour, and little routine. In other lower-skilled companies and sectors with predominantly routine jobs and relatively unskilled workers, labour's flexibility is based on the ease of its replacement. This reflects the fact that wage relations are not widely generalized. Such duality – dubbed Toyotism – includes competition from above and from below that is better able to preserve the unity between production and capital circulation. This has contributed to the relative success of these countries and firms in the new international division of labour (ibid.: 11–27).

Amid the growing exclusion and instability affecting labour around the world, there are no signs of a new trend that would reconnect money with the real economy. The amount of resources destined to physical investment is decreasing, while financial investment continues to climb (CEPII, 1996: 196–9). Mergers, acquisitions, privatizations, and all types of auctions rather than fresh investments, dominate the global market. Latin America is no exception. Roustang et al. state that in the last instance 'a (growing) part of national income is not invested or consumed, but used instead to finance the increased capitalization of the stock exchange' (1996: 50).

This trend leads to economic involution that continues to intensify as long as there is an inability to regulate international demand effectively.

Gambling on the future has increased with time. Transnational corporations, big banks, pension funds and so on are no longer the only players in the stock market. Families, especially in North America and Europe, even mortgage their homes to take part in the global casino (*The Economist*, 1996: 114). Under these circumstances, the last gamblers seem to have placed their bets in the game. The big institutional gamblers are looking to cash in their winnings, and it is increasingly difficult to maintain rising expectations. Sooner or later this will lead to capital losing its gamble on the future, thus to a worldwide money crisis. The inability to regulate production and money will finally lead to a global collapse of the financial system. Today, money's future is virtually up in the air (Cleaver, 1995: 39, 57).

3

Globalization: The Origin of Borderless Private States

Globalization: Towards a No-growth Economy

Since the Second World War, two major periods have led to the international economic interdependence that characterizes globalization. The first was a time of steady growth brought on by reconstruction efforts based on clear state intervention to stimulate the productive sectors. Strong productive investment and sustained growth through state intervention fostered increasing involvement that lasted until the late 1960s and early 1970s. In the second period, investments gradually abandoned the productive sphere to become more transnational. This trend is apparent in the global integration of financial capital and in the rise of foreign direct investment (FDI) that was displaced towards nonproductive sectors. It is a period of economic stagnation, with declining average rates of gain and longer and more frequent recessions. The social welfare state was dismantled, thus leading to greater exclusion and concentration of capital in the hands of transnationals (Dierckxsens, 1995: 151–60). This topic will be explored further in Chapter 4.

The first period involved extended reproduction of productive capital and stimulation of economic growth. The second emphasized mechanisms for the redistribution and concentration of existing wealth rather than the creation of wealth. Maximization of profits prevailed on a micro level, disproportionately channelling investment towards those nonproductive sectors that do not create wealth. It is a paradox that the benefits from productive sectors tend to be lower than the average profits in the economy as a whole, while benefits obtained outside productive sectors are higher. Without state intervention, the

Table 3.1 FDI: source countries and recipients, 1970–97

Countries and sectors	1970	1975	1980 (billion dollars)	1985	1990	1997	1970	1975	1980 (distribution %)	1985	1990	1997
'Outward stock'												
Developed countries												
Primary	29	58	88	115	160	–	22.7	25.3	18.5	18.5	11.2	–
Secondary	58	103	208	240	556	–	45.2	45.0	43.8	37.7	38.7	–
Tertiary	41	68	179	265	720	–	31.4	27.7	37.7	42.8	50.1	–
Total	128	229	475	620	1,436	2,945	100.0	100.0	100.0	100.0	100.0	–
'Inward stock'												
Developed countries												
Primary	12	17	18	39	94	165	16.2	12.1	6.7	9.2	9.1	8.0
Secondary	44	79	148	195	439	660	60.2	56.5	55.2	46.2	42.5	32.0
Tertiary	17	44	102	188	499	1,235	23.7	31.4	38.1	44.5	48.4	60.0
Total	73	140	268	422	1,032	2,060	100.0	100.0	100.0	100.0	100.0	100.0
Underdeveloped countries												
Primary	–	7	17	31	46	97	–	20.6	22.7	24.0	21.9	7.0
Secondary	–	19	41	64	102	787	–	55.9	54.6	49.6	48.6	57.0
Tertiary	–	8	17	34	62	496	–	23.5	22.7	26.4	29.5	36.0
Total	–	34	75	129	210	1,380	–	100.0	100.0	100.0	100.0	100.0

Source: UNCTAD, *Transnational Corporations*, 2 (2) (August 1993): 111; for 1997 UNCTAD 1999: 12.

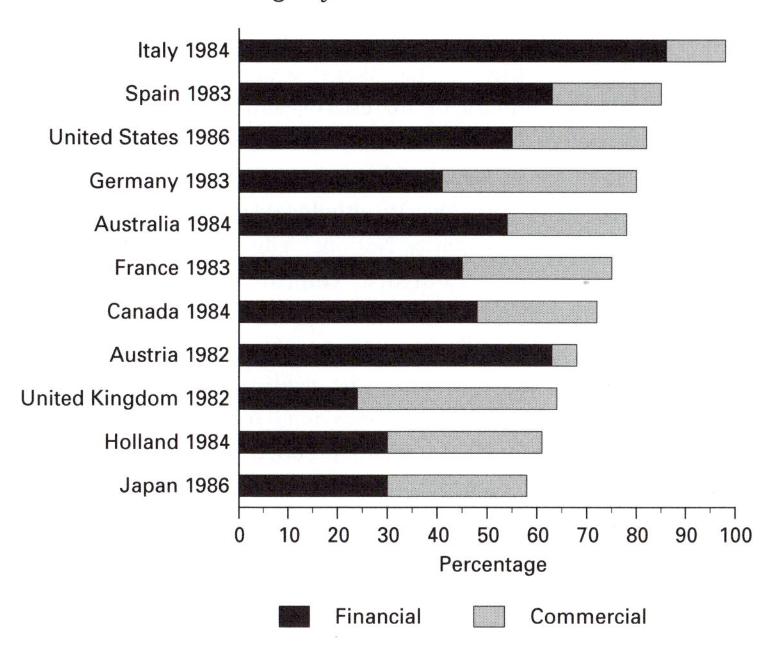

Figure 3.1 Financial and commercial sector shares of FDI (%)
(*Source*: Dierckxsens, 1994: 154)

'invisible hand' thus tends towards underinvestment in productive sectors, discouraging creation of wealth and obstructing economic dynamism (see Table 3.1). It tends to concentrate investment in transaction activities (commercial and financial investments) that energize the (re)distribution and appropriation of existing wealth, thus indirectly promoted by redistribution policies favouring lower incomes (see Figure 3.1). While nonproductive investments favour higher incomes at the expense of lower ones, they also tend to contract demand and deter the indirect promotion of production. They become increasingly autonomous and thus more speculative, curbing economic dynamism.

This open 'invisible hand' tends to increase efficiency on a micro level but does not provide greater well-being for everyone. Increased micro-level efficiency does not lead to efficiency at a macro level: quite the contrary. The problem lies in confusing profit and wealth. On a micro level it would seem that regardless of their content, all units of production or of service, create profit, value and wealth as long as that product or service is paid for and makes a profit. According to this perspective all unpaid labour – such as domestic labour – does not create wealth due to the very fact that it is unpaid. Regardless of its usefulness and the amount of material wealth it represents, unpaid labour is not included in national bookkeeping and is not taken into account as labour or as wealth. This perspective sees wealth defined by its form or social relation. Wealth includes that which can be counted or expressed monetarily. National ledgers include the sum of all individual monetary wealth that, compared over time, indicate economic growth.

As investment is channelled towards nonproductive spheres, wealth tends to grow more slowly and must be divided as remuneration. The average profits from investments thus tend to decrease. When investment is not rechannelled towards production, the result is more aggressive micro-level competition and less intervention to increase participation in a slow-growth market. Transnational capital thus seeks to increase its competitive edge through investments that improve its strategic position in the world market. For example, FDI that promotes concentration rather than creation of wealth is that involved in acquiring companies with existing markets and clientele. These acquisitions, often based on credit, create expectations that market success will bring real future profits, thus leading stock prices to exceed their real values and stimulating speculation. History teaches that in the medium term this trend leads to the need for a 'visible hand' that is strong enough to make investment return to production with greater involvement.

Development of Borderless Private Consortiums in the Triad

Globalization involves an economic dispute for the world market waged by transnational corporations from the Triad: the United States, the European Union (EU) and Japan. No longer are these transnationals merely commodity exporters. In this battle, FDI produces a web of properties that transcend borders. Production and distribution of goods and services are restructured less among nations and more among 'borderless private consortiums'. 'The *made in* label ... tends to be replaced with *made by*' (Andreff, 1995: 59). FDIs are essentially those by transnational corporations, and they originate in a handful of countries. In 1990, 90% of FDI came from just nine countries: the

G-7 – the United States, Canada, Germany, France, Great Britain, Italy and Japan – plus Switzerland and the Netherlands. Another 5% came from other industrialized countries and the remaining 5% from the rest of the world (ILO, 1993: 293).

The impact of this worldwide restructuring through FDI depends on its relative volume. In the context of today's world economy, the relative importance of national economies is increasingly overshadowed by that of transnational corporations (TNCs) and their FDI. A 1990 survey of 37,530 TNCs from primary, secondary and tertiary sectors found that their total sales represented 50% of the world's GDP, while in 1992 the largest 200 generated 27% (Andreff, 1995: 77). In 1994, for example, the combined incomes of the 500 largest TNCs was US$10,245 million, equivalent that same year to the total GDP of the USA, Japan and Germany. That was almost 75% of the G-7's GDP and one-fourth of the total world production (Chomsky and Dietrich, 1995: 49; CEPII, 1995: 108). The combined profits of the five hundred largest TNCs in 1994 came to US$282 billion, surpassing the growth of the G-7's GDP (in US dollars). In 1995, FDI by transnationals reached the even greater sum of US$325 billion.

Increasingly, economic integration can be measured less by the flow of trade between nations. Since the 1980s with the exponential growth of FDI, the more direct TNC-led economic integration has become increasingly important. This can be measured by relating a country's GDP to the sum of the aggregate value generated by TNCs based in that country and that generated by its TNCs abroad. In the early 1990s this was 50% greater than the GDP of smaller core countries such as Canada, Switzerland, the Netherlands, Belgium and even Great Britain. It was 30% greater for countries such as Germany, France, Australia, and Italy, and 20% greater for the United States and Japan (Dunning, 1992: 12). The presence of TNCs was felt first in the smaller-scale core economies, but as FDI increased they came to dominate the economies of the industrialized nations and of the entire world. Exports accounted for one-half of all TNCs' sales: they generated over 50% of US exports, over 80% of those of the UK and over 90% of Singapore's (Andreff, 1995: 79).

FDI has skyrocketed in the last ten years (see Figure 3.2,), averaging more than US$125 billion a year. This represents slightly less than one-half of the G-7's absolute growth in dollars. FDI existed prior to

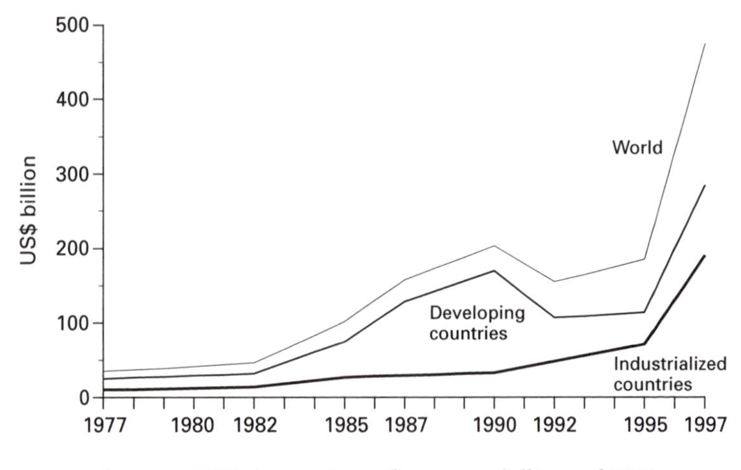

Figure 3.2 FDI: destinations of, 1977–95 (billions of US$) (*Source*: OIT, 1995 and IRELA, 1996: 107)

the 1970s, as did TNCs' integration across national borders. FDI has gradually increased since that time and grew exponentially throughout the 1980s, as illustrated in Figure 3.2. The FDI boom in the 1980s primarily involved the major Triad nations. Over 75% of FDI was made within that triangle of world economic power, and only 20% in peripheral countries. One per cent of locally based TNCs in each industrialized country was responsible for 50% of its FDI abroad (Andreff, 1995: 77).

In 1990, 40% of FDI within the Triad (excluding that among EU countries) crossed the Atlantic, while 40% crossed the Pacific and the remaining 20% was between the EU and Japan (see Figure 3.3). At first glance this would place the United States front and centre. A second glance reveals imbalances among the three major powers. Fifty-six per cent of recent FDI came from Japan, while the United States received 61% of these intra-Triad investments. This illustrates how the TNC web is increasingly spun from Japan to the USA. The 'borderless private consortiums' are moving to Japan and acting on the United States. This trend threatens US national sovereignty and the TNCs headquartered there.

In the economic dispute for world markets, foreign investment is directed towards improving competitive positions rather than productive endeavours. Therefore, FDI are increasingly concentrated in

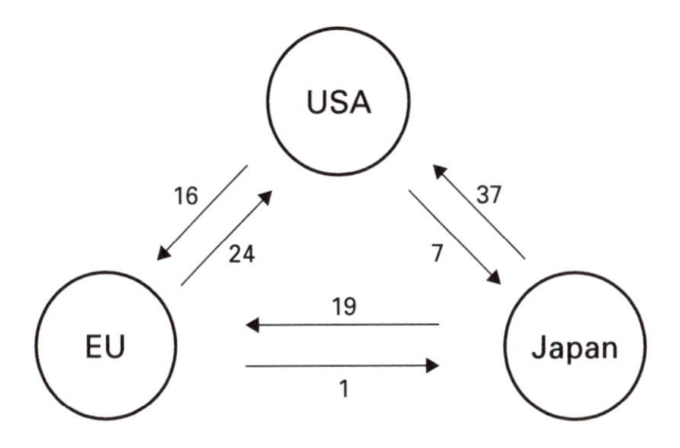

Figure 3.3 FDI within the Triad, 1990 (*Source*: UNCTAD, *Transnational Corporations in World Development*, several issues)

the service sector, especially transaction services. In the 1950s, 80% of FDI was made in the primary and secondary sectors. In the late 1980s approximately 50% of these investments were in services and almost 80% of these in commercial and financial services (UN Centre on Transnational Corporations, 1988: 366, 370, 383). TNC acquisitions represent an important segment of these nonproductive investments. Between 1984 and 1988, 75% of FDI in the United States was for mergers and acquisitions. Between 1989 and 1990 acquisitions accounted for over 50% of FDI in the EU (ILO, 1993: 299).

The general shift of investments – particularly FDI – towards nonproductive activities has diminished the economic dynamism of the Triad and the world. Between 1966 and 1973 productive investment was predominant. The annual growth rate of the world economy reached 5%. It fell to 3.5% in the late 1970s and continued its gradual decline in the 1980s until reaching slightly more than 1% in the 1990s. Per capita growth of the GDP further illustrates the anaemia of today's world economy, as shown in Tables 3.2 and 3.3.

The productive nature of investments within the Triad differs depending on the direction of its flows. Strong Japanese investment in the United States is more concentrated in nonproductive activities (acquisitions) than is weaker US investment in Japan. Its historic roots include Japan's hostility to foreign investment until 1970. After the OECD forced the Japanese to open their borders, formal barriers were replaced by informal ones through so-called stock cross-holdings among groups of Japanese corporations. These policies made acquisi-

Table 3.2 The world economy by principal region

Regions	Pop. in mill. of inhab. 1992	GDP in US$ billions 1992	Per capita GDP 1992	AYPG[1] of pop. 1979–92	AYPG of GDP 1979–92	AYPG per capita GDP 1979–92	Per capita GDP growth (%)		
							1990	1991	1992
World	5,414	29,814	5,626	1.7	2.6	0.9	0.2	-1.6	-0.1
North America	283	6,472	22,903	1.0	2.1	1.1	-0.2	-2.3	1.5
Western Europe	469	6,979	14,897	0.9	2.3	1.5	2.0	-0.7	-0.2
European Union	347	5,898	16,991	0.7	2.3	1.8	2.3	-1.1	0.2
Former USSR and Eastern Europe	372	2,271	6,107	0.7	-1.6	-1.9	-5.8	-18.1	-13.7
Middle East and Maghreb[2]	258	1,185	4,599	3.2	1.4	-1.7	0.8	0.0	1.2
Sub-Saharan Africa	487	550	1,131	2.9	2.3	-0.6	1.0	-0.1	1.0
South Africa	45	184	4,209	2.6	2.0	-0.6	-2.5	-2.5	-0.2
Latin America	454	2,727	6,008	2.0	1.8	-0.2	-1.5	1.4	1.4
Dynamic Eastern economies[3]	523	4,606	8,819	1.5	4.9	3.3	4.3	3.7	2.3
China and Indonesia	1,250	2,952	2,530	1.5	8.3	6.7	3.6	5.5	6.7
Indian subcontinent[4]	1,219	1,502	1,232	2.2	5.3	3.1	3.2	0.2	2.3
Oceania	29	384	14,285	1.6	2.6	1.1	-1.9	-0.9	1.2

Notes: 1. AYPG = average yearly percentage growth. 2. The Middle East and Maghreb include Algeria, Saudi Arabia, Egypt, Iraq, Iran, Morocco and Syria. 3. Dynamic Eastern economies include Hong Kong, Indonesia, South Korea, Japan and Malaysia. 4. The Indian subcontinent includes Bangladesh, India, Burma and Pakistan.

Source: CEPII, 1994: 12.

Table 3.3 World output, growth in 1966–93 (percentage of average annual growth of GDP at market prices and 1987 exchange rates)

	1966–73	1974–80	1981–90	1991–93
World total	4.9	3.5	3.3	1.1
Developed countries	4.7	3.2	3.2	1.2
Eastern Europe and Central Asia	7.0	4.5	2.3	-9.8
Developing countries	6.4	4.8	3.6	4.6
East Asia	8.0	7.0	7.9	8.3
China	8.9	6.3	9.9	11.2
Southern Asia	3.6	3.9	5.6	3.5
Sub-Saharan Africa	5.0	4.0	1.9	1.7
Latin America and the Caribbean	6.8	4.8	2.0	3.2
Middle East and North Africa	7.0	4.6	0.4	3.0

Source: ILO, 1995: 32.

tions more difficult by requiring the concurrent purchase of stocks from other companies. Greenfield investments (real new investments) were practically the only option and represented 66% of FDI in Japan. Important Japanese acquisitions in the United States did not bring growth to that country. On the other hand, lower US investment in Japan had a weak but positive effect on Japanese economic growth (Lawrence, 1992: 50, 59, 63).

Growth rates of production and world trade were negatively affected by the economic expansion of TNCs through intra-Triad FDI. Between 1974 and 1983 world trade increased by 8.9% annually, slowing to a mere 3% per year in the next five years. It became even more anaemic in the early 1990s (see Table 3.4). North–North trade became increasingly important between 1979 and 1992 as a result of this slowing economic growth. It accounted for more than half of all world trade, while South–North trade fell by 20%, clearly demonstrating the North's protectionism as illustrated in Table 3.5. During that same period, North–South trade grew to 20%, revealing lower protectionism and greater penetration of the South. South–South trade fell to less than 10% of the world total.

In the 1980s, which were characterized by decreasing growth and average rates of gain, intra-Triad FDI was used to strengthen the competitive positions of TNCs and allow them to acquire a greater

Table 3.4 World trade, growth in, 1950–94 (percentage of average annual growth)

	1950–73	1974–83	1984–89	1990	1991–94
World trade[1] volume	7.7	3.1	6.4	4.6	3.8
Value	n.d.	8.9	3.0	8.3	-0.7
Volume of exports					
Industrial countries	n.d.	3.9	5.9	5.8	2.8
Transition economies[2]	n.d.	3.6	2.4	-9.5	-15.0
Developing countries	n.d.	-1.9	7.3	8.7	8.2
Four recently industrialized Asian countries	n.d.	-0.6	2.4	7.7	2.8
Sub-Saharan Africa	n.d.	-0.6	2.4	7.7	2.8
Imports					
Industrial countries	n.d.	2.8	7.9	4.8	2.9
Transition economies	n.d.	2.2	2.9	-5.1	-13.5
Developing countries	n.d.	7.0	3.3	5.5	11.2
Four recently industrialized Asian countries	n.d.	9.0	13.2	12.5	12.0
Sub-Saharan Africa	n.d.	-0.5	0.9	1.8	-2.4

Notes: 1. Average of percentages of variations in world exports and imports: includes peripheral and industrialized countries' trade and that of transition economies except trade with the former USSR. 2. Eastern Europe and the former USSR.

Source: ILO, 1995: 35.

share of the stagnant pie. The Japanese were able to gain a competitive edge in the world market by weaving better networks. In 1979 before the strong wave of foreign investment, the USA was responsible for 44% of intra-Triad exports, Japan for 25%, and the EU (excluding exports within the Union) for the remaining 33%. This demonstrates the United States' relative dominance. The competitive positions of the major powers within the Triad shifted with the primary wave of investment. Between 1979 and 1992 exports from the USA – the primary recipient of FDI – fell eight points to 36%. The EU also lost ground, falling to 30%. Japan was the big winner: its exports increased by nine points to become 34% of intra-Triad exports.

Strong FDI by TNCs throughout the Triad leads to increased intra-

Table 3.5 All exports, 1979 and 1992 compared (per thousand of total change)

Recipient source		North America	Western Europe	Japan	Developing Asia	Latin America	Arab World	Sub-Saharan Africa	Eastern Europe	World
North America	1979	47	36	14	13	19	7	1	4	147
	1992	51	35	15	21	21	5	1	2	154
Western Europe	1979	30	309	5	16	14	32	12	19	450
	1992	34	346	9	23	10	19	6	17	477
Japan	1979	18	10	0	19	4	7	2	2	64
	1992	29	20	0	33	4	4	1	1	94
Developing Asia	1979	17	15	17	14	2	5	1	3	75
	1992	33	26	20	34	3	5	1	3	129
Latin America	1979	20	13	2	1	10	4	1	3	56
	1992	20	10	2	2	8	1	0	1	45
Arab World	1979	17	43	16	7	4	5	0	3	96
	1992	4	16	7	7	1	4	0	1	40
Sub-Saharan Africa	1979	7	11	1	1	2	1	1	0	25
	1992	3	5	0	0	0	0	1	0	11
Eastern Europe	1979	1	21	1	2	3	3	0	26	58
	1992	1	16	1	3	0	1	0	5	26
World	1979	160	471	61	77	54	65	20	61	1,000
	1992	178	482	58	130	48	39	11	29	1,000

Source: CEPII, 1994: Table 4.

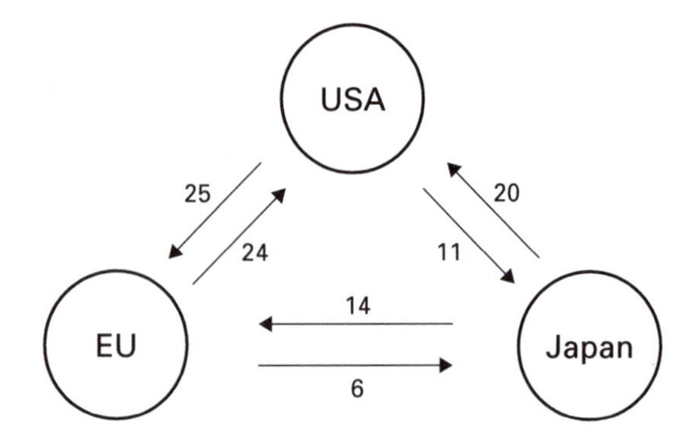

Figure 3.4 Trade within the Triad, 1992 (*Source*: CEPII, 1994)

corporate transactions. In 1991 Japanese FDI funds in the USA were four times those of the USA in Japan (ILO, 1993: 13). As a result, two-way FDI intra-corporate transactions accounted for 50% of trade between Japan and the USA (Ostry, 1992: 9). In 1992 such transactions accounted for approximately 40% of world trade (Chomsky and Dietrich, 1995: 49). This is not trade in the true sense, but distribution of the product of private centralized global planning. TNCs have become 'borderless private states'. Their private planning has increased production both at the expense of and in the heart of the market economy. Private planning in postcapitalism is gaining ground at the expense of the market economy (Goldsmith, 1996: 19).

Economic disputes between TNCs arise from efforts to use FDI to improve their positions in the rest of the world market. Their standing is largely determined by effectively structured foreign investments. This world market dispute within the Triad began in the early 1980s. By the end of the decade, Japan emerged as the victorious power, leaving the USA behind (see Figure 3.4). More strategic placement of foreign investments allowed Japan to improve its competitive position within the Triad at the expense of the United States. The US TNCs lost ground in the world market as their FDI structure became less effective, leading to their special interest in avoiding further losses (Morrison and Roth, 1992: 37). The answer is twofold. Economic blocs built in the early 1990s obstruct intra-Triad FDI and benefit the periphery. Following the Mexican crisis, the United States has taken the lead as the major FDI recipient and investor in acquisitions in the

Triad. Between 1994 and 1995 the withdrawal of FDI from the United States and Germany doubled. The economic dispute intensified and FDI in the North went from US$128 to US$228 billion in 1995.

Borderless Private States and Economic Blocs

Trade and FDI shifts within the Triad favouring Japan over the United States have caused friction, especially between the two nations. Neo-protectionist measures affecting trade and foreign investment have been expanded. There has been worry over a 1930s-style depression. The Uruguay Round of the GATT promoted opening world trade to avoid increased protectionism and the resulting economic collapse of the more industrialized countries.

The Uruguay Round dismantled tariff barriers at a time when the major powers were using non-tariff measures such as quotas, social and ecological conditions, and quality controls. Intellectual property rights were introduced as another new barrier to obstruct competition from the South. Participants agreed to disagree regarding advanced technology such as aerospace, aviation and audiovisual, and over financial issues regulating North–North competition. This led to neo-protectionism in the North at the same time the South was opening up. The disintegration of the Soviet bloc made possible the division of the peripheral world among major TNCs without any real social or political difficulties. Globalization has led to *laissez faire* policies for the South as well as regionalization and the formation of diverse economic blocs (see Lawrence, 1992: 73; Buelens, 1995: 518).

The unfettered flow of FDI to the periphery and the division of the peripheral world among the major powers began in the early 1990s at the expense of North–North investments (see Figure 1.1 and Figure 3.6). In years past, dividing up the world required territorial occupation and these shifts often led to international upheaval. Commercial and financial integration has made it more economical to subject peripheral countries to transnational capital. Monetary control initiatives, along with conditions concerning foreign debt that were imposed on peripheral countries, clearly led to their indirect subjection to transnational capital and the loss of self-determination. FDI signalled a shift from indirect to direct subordination of the periphery to transnational capital.

Table 3.6 FDI recipients in Latin America, 1988–98 (net amounts in millions of US$ and as percentage of totals)

	1988	1990	1992	1994	1998
World	156,809	201,485	162,130	215,508	644,000
Industrialized countries	132,056	169,687	113,221	128,267	460,460
Developing countries	24,753	31,798	48,909	87,241	243,540
Africa[1]	1,364	1,112	2,200	3,214	7,728
Southeast Asia	12,593	18,302	25,607	50,178	99,820
Europe[2]	472	1,156	4,555	6,022	1,288
Middle East	1,532	3,170	2,063	3,385	3,220
Latin America and the Caribbean[3]	8,792	8,058	14,484	24,442	71,484
World	100	100	100	100	100
Industrialized countries	84.2	84.2	69.8	59.5	71.5
Developing countries	15.8	15.8	30.2	40.5	28.5
Africa[1]	0.9	0.6	1.4	1.5	1.2
Southeast Asia	8.0	9.1	15.8	23.3	15.5
Europe[2]	0.3	0.6	2.8	2.8	0.2
Middle East	1.0	1.6	1.3	1.6	0.5
Latin America and the Caribbean[3]	5.6	4.0	8.9	11.3	11.1

Notes: 1. Africa includes the entire continent except Libya and Egypt. 2. Europe includes Central and Eastern European countries, Cyprus, Malta and Turkey. 3. Latin America and the Caribbean refers to the Western Hemisphere.

Source: IRELA, 1996: 107; UNCTAD, 1999: 18.

FDI in the periphery does not benefit all countries, nor is it determined by chance. It is channelled primarily to the faster-growing emergent economies of Asia. Table 3.5 illustrates that increased FDI in the 1990s – due largely to investment in Asia – represented 58% of all FDI in peripheral countries in 1994. That same year China, an emergent market with enormous potential, attracted one-fourth of all FDI in the periphery (ILO, 1995: 50). In the early 1990s, almost 45% of FDI went to three primary recipients – China, Singapore and Mexico. In contrast, Africa and the Middle East each represented a mere 6% of the FDI for all peripheral countries (see Table 3.5). Investment was channelled to some peripheral nations and excluded many others, even entire subcontinents.

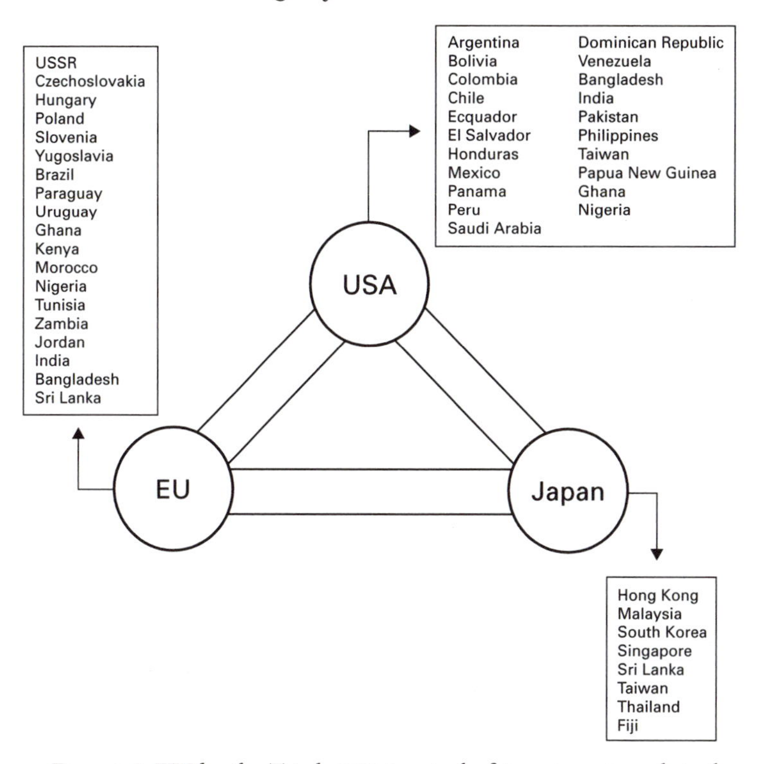

Figure 3.5 FDI by the Triad, 1990 (control of investments and stocks by Triad members) (*Source*: UNCTAD, 1993: 119)

Although Europeans and North Americans also invested in Asia, and Europeans and Japanese invested in Latin America, there was clear regionalization of FDI among the powers. The strong wave of FDI in the 1990s illustrates this trend and the imposition of US hegemony in Latin America, Japanese in Asia, and that of the EU in Central Europe and the East. While between 1985 and 1989 a full 54% of FDI in Latin America came from Europe and only 40% from the USA, between 1990 and 1995 the USA provided 74% and European participation dropped to a mere 22%. Japan's role in the continent has been marginal and continues to decrease (see IRELA, 1996: 109). These FDI flows towards the neighbouring regions of each of the three powers gave rise to three economic blocs, each dominated by one of the members of the Triad, as shown in Figure 3.5.

Latin America: Private States and Economic Blocs

FDI in Asia is not characterized by the same North–South flows as in Latin America or by the triangulation found in the Asian Pacific. Although Japan is the region's primary investor, this is not true individually for each of the eastern countries. Taiwan is dominant in Malaysia, South Korea in Indonesia, and Hong Kong in China, although Japan is strongly represented in each. Japan is the majority holder of direct foreign investments in the region as a whole (Margolin, 1994: 93). East–East FDI is clearly on the rise, strengthening Asian Pacific integration under Japanese hegemony. Japanese investment in Asia increased from US$6.6 billion in 1994 to US$9.7 billion in 1995, a relative increase of 47% (OECD, 1995: 130).

FDI in Asia are channelled in second place to productive activities, particularly industry (ILO, 1995: 50). Foreign investment in Asian industry is directed towards exports and complements domestic savings-based investments in industry. Between 1993 and 1996, both contributed to the growth of this sector, from 10% per year in South Korea to 20% per year in China (see Table 3.7). This strong tendency towards productive investment developed a new engine of the world economy, greatly increasing exports to the USA and the EU between 1979 and 1992 and exceeding their exports to the 'Tigers' as illustrated in Table 3.4. The West's basically defensive Eastern strategy aimed to avoid losing further competitive advantage.

The Asian Pacific's incorporation into the world economy was based on its competitive advantage following integration, a process originating in the East–West conflict. Western policies promoting models meant to overshadow neighbouring socialist economies led to the integration of the 'Tigers' or 'Dragons of the East' – Hong Kong, South Korea, Taiwan and Singapore – into the world economy. To this end, major powers, such as the United States and Japan, deliberately opened their markets to these smaller nations, allowing these economies to replace their import substitution policies with export promotion (Millán, 1992: 31–4).

The end of the Cold War brought an end to any political mediation to provide other Southern nations with such opportunities. It actually led to tougher positions regarding greater competition from the Tigers. Protecting intellectual property rights though the GATT's Uruguay

Round helps to prevent new Dragons from emerging in the South. Asian Pacific economic integration is largely the result of the Tigers' loss of their former preferential status due to increased protectionism by the industrialized economies. This regional integration, which is able to compete on a global scale, is also a two-way process that assumes relative equality among member states. Two-way trade and FDI characterize the Tigers' integration process. As a group they are recipients of FDI and they also invest in other parts of the world.

Asian Pacific integration is evident as well in the growing trade within the region. In 1992, 42% of Taiwan's exports and 47% of its imports were regional, compared to 30% and 40% in 1986. Japan's second, third and fourth largest clients were Hong Kong (and thus China), Taiwan, and South Korea. China was its second largest supplier (Adda, 1994: 92).

The region's economic integration is based on financial and commercial triangulation, which has intensified along with the North's increasing protectionism. Less developed countries whose industries are based on import substitution have been included in the 1990s: Indonesia, the Philippines, Malaysia and Thailand. These are countries with significant foreign debts. They are hardly able to participate as equals. It has become a process of regionalization rather than integration.

Latin America is experiencing a similar process of regionalization without integration. In the spirit of article 24 of the GATT, economic integration was meant to be an intermediate stage leading to global free trade. It was to include free trade zones and customs unions. Integration processes developed following this model – including the diverse experiences in Latin America – are based on the idea that it is possible only among neighbouring countries sharing similar levels of development. The European Union is an example of this among the developed countries. As was also the case with the Asian Pacific, it was founded on strictly political rather than economic grounds. Following the two world wars, the customs union was meant to prevent another military conflict in the European household (Lennep, 1995: 508). In recent years a new 'regionality' built on the EU's foundations has come to include countries with different levels of development such as those in Central and Eastern Europe and the Mediterranean nations (Osa, 1996: 7–12).

Table 3.7 Growth in GDP and manufacturing, Latin America and the Asian Tigers compared, 1993–96 (annual percentage of change)

	GDP	Ind. prod.
Latin America: 6 emergent economies		
Chile	5.9	7.9
Brazil	4.5	6.0
Argentina	2.5	1.2
Mexico	1.4	3.4
Colombia	-4.0	-1.1
Venezuela	-4.3	n.a.
Non-weighted average	2.8	4.1
Asia: 6 economies		
China	11.0	19.5
Malaysia	9.5	12.3
Singapore	9.4	11.4
South Korea	7.9	9.8
Thailand	7.9	10.1
Indonesia	6.9	13.1
Non-weighted average	8.7	12.8

Source: *The Economist*, economic indicators for January 1994, June 1995 and May 1996.

Integration processes in the various Latin American common markets have not led to the development of mini-blocs. On the contrary: following the foreign debt crisis, the relative weakness of these markets in the globalized world has forced them to open to hegemonic blocs. Rather than consolidating a regionality that was built on internal integration, structural adjustment policies have imposed a shift towards open regionality at the expense of internal integration (CEPAL, 1994 in Osa, 1996). These countries have had to open their markets to all sorts of industrial goods from hegemonic blocs, seriously damaging their own industrialization. Openness to foreign goods and investment from the dominant blocs prevail in the region. In this context, industry is based on FDI – maquila. The simultaneous combination of both processes has not promoted internal productive investment or economic growth, as illustrated in Table 3.7.

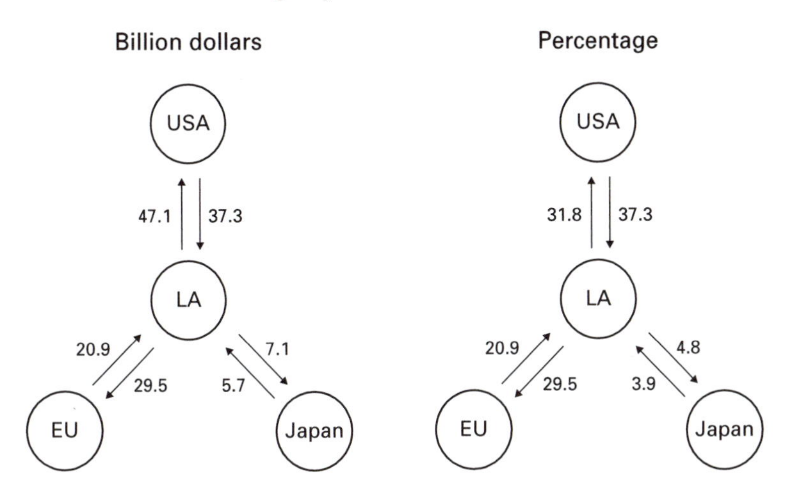

Figure 3.6 Latin American trade with the Triad, 1990
(*Source*: IRELA, 1996: 103)

The incorporation of the periphery in the global regionalization of the 1990s, and specifically that of Latin America, was driven by an external dynamic. Figures 3.6 and 3.7 show that Latin American trade grew by 74% between 1990 and 1994. However, imports were the most dynamic segment as these countries opened their markets to goods from the major powers. These imports, primarily industrial goods, increased by 116% in that period. This was three times greater than the 42% increase in exports, mostly nonindustrial products. The region lost its positive balance of trade with the Triad and with each of the three superpowers. US hegemony over trade in the hemisphere was established as its participation increased from 57% to 64%. The EU's share dropped from 34% to 28% of the hemisphere's trade with the Triad. Japan was the minority partner; its share fell from 9% to 8%. FDI was similarly affected: intense FDI compensated for the unfavourable balance of trade caused by foreign debt. Between 1990 and 1994 Latin America received a total of US$46 billion in direct investment, four times greater than between 1985 and 1989. During this latter period, most FDI in the region – 54% – still came from Europe. In the first half of the 1990s, however, US investment greatly exceeded European: 74% versus 22% (see Table 3.9).

Since 1990, the USA has channelled most of its FDI in Latin America

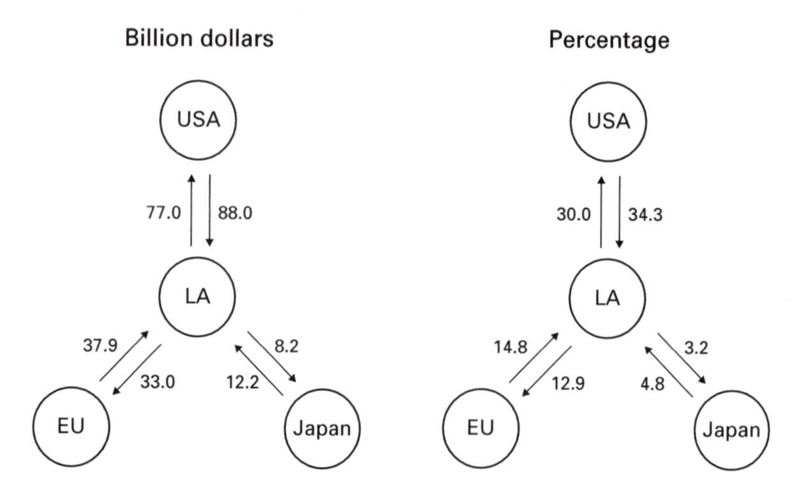

Figure 3.7 Latin American trade with the Triad, 1994
(*Source*: IRELA, 1996: 103)

to Brazil and Mexico, each receiving one-third of the total. Argentina, Colombia and Chile are other major recipients. US businesses began investing strongly in Mexico even before the North American Free Trade Agreement (NAFTA). In 1994 Brazil surpassed Mexico as the recipient of the most US FDI; they received US$3.5 billion and US$3.3 billion respectively. With this spectacular direct investment in Brazil the US exceeded the especially strong European investment made in that country. In general, the United States has been the main source of FDI for all subregional groups throughout the 1990s (see Table 3.9). FDI has been channelled primarily towards certain countries. Smaller countries tend to receive more modest amounts even though their per capita amounts might exceed those of larger countries. In 1994, the per capita FDI by the EU in Uruguay and Costa Rica was much greater than in Brazil, which was the biggest recipient (IRELA, 1996: 37, 110). A chain is created as the region's largest countries are opened to goods from the superpowers receiving FDI in return, and the smaller countries are opened to goods from the region's larger nations in exchange for their FDI. In this sense, the Mexican economy has become North Americanized, and the Central American economy has become Mexicanized.

This massive chronic trade imbalance depends on a strong stable

Table 3.8 FDI in Latin America and the Caribbean, 1980–94 (net amounts, in US$ millions)

Annual average	1980/84	1985/89	1990/94	1990	1992	1994
EU	1,176	1,265	1,952	1,730	1,398	4,446
USA	1,263	941	6,732	3,217	5,568	11,582
Japan	435	149	386	399	270	568
Totals	2,874	2,355	9,200	5,346	7,236	16,757

Source: IRELA, 1996: 109.

Table 3.9 FDI in Latin America, by source and recipient regions

Recipient	1990–94: source in %				In US$ millions		
	USA	EU	Japan	Total	1990–94	1985–89	1980–84
Latin America	74	22	4	100	9,070	2,325	2,873
Andean Group	63	33	4	100	1,225	-406	417
Central America	82	16	2	100	106	31	56
Group of Three	83	11	6	100	3,579	260	782
Mercosur	72	24	4	100	4,034	1,933	1,724

Source: IRELA, 1996: 109–14.

flow of capital to the region. Table 3.10 shows that between 1988 and 1994 Latin America received 50% of all foreign investment compared to Asia's 35%. The main difference is that foreign investment in Latin America is much less stable than in Asia, as 75% are securities investments. In Asia, on the other hand, 75% are FDI. Investment in short-term securities (interest differences) causes highly speculative capital flows that can be quickly reversed. This occurred in the Mexican crisis in 1995 when there was a net withdrawal of US$17 billion in securities capital from Mexico. This gigantic withdrawal was partly compensated for by unprecedented injections of financial resources by the US government itself and by multilateral lending agencies. New monetary initiatives are aimed at halting the massive introduction of short-term securities capital by reducing interest rates in the region. Long-term capital flows, especially FDI, are encouraged (see Table 3.10). Privatization of state-owned businesses is an important priority.

Table 3.10 FDI, type of and recipient regions globally, 1988–97 (in US$ billions and percentage of total)

	1984–89		1994		1995		1996		1997	
	Portfolio	FDI	Portfolio	FDI	Portfolio	FDI	Portfolio	FDI	Portfolio	FDI
Developing countries	4.7	13.1	83.8	78.9	20.6	82.8	47.5	101.8	35.6	120.0
Africa	-0.8	1.1	0.5	3.6	1.4	4.2	-0.3	5.3	2.6	7.7
Asia	2.0	5.5	10.1	46.9	10.8	48.2	14.8	55.3	-7.2	56.0
Middle East	4.4	1.1	12.5	4.2	8.4	5.1	7.9	4.3	6.8	5.1
Latin America	-0.9	5.3	60.6	24.3	-0.1	25.3	25.2	36.9	33.5	51.2

Source: ILO, 1999: 13.

The spectacular decline of US exports to Mexico in 1995 following the crash of the Mexican peso was accompanied by a sharp rise in imports and consequently opposition to NAFTA within the United States. Regionalization was not interrupted but was shown to carry economic risks for investors and political problems for neighbours. FDI and regionalization have been redefined and further separated from geographic borders. In 1995, Brazil experienced a spectacular rise in imports from the US and the EU, along with an enormous wave of FDI. FDI rather than geographic vicinity now determines the dynamic of participation in the world economy. After the Mexican crisis FDI in the periphery actually increased from US$87 billion in 1994 to US$97 billion in 1995. North–North flows were even greater, however, increasing from US$128 billion to US$228 billion (IRELA, 1996). Since 1995 the Triad has again become TNCs' primary battlefield. Although the periphery has not been abandoned, there is less emphasis on consolidating regions.

The cause of the surprising 1997 speculative crisis in Southeast Asia lies neither in Asia nor in a handful of unscrupulous speculators, but in the economic world war that has broken out among major TNCs over a global market that does not have room for all. Asia's monetary crisis began slightly earlier than that of Hong Kong with an apparently isolated attack on the Thai currency, which was being bombarded by speculators. A deterioration of the country's balance of payments alerted Thailand to the devaluation. The situation was repeated in Malaysia. The United States did not help these countries as it had Mexico during the 1994–95 crisis. The USA was able to use this Asian crisis to bring the region under the control of the International Monetary Fund (IMF) and to open its very protected markets (Sender, 1997: 69). We will return to this topic in Chapter 5.

4

Globalization: The Creation of a World Labour Market

Introduction

In a market economy citizenship – true membership in a given nation and the related social rights – is largely determined by the population's level of involvement in market relations. This in turn largely depends on how widespread wage relations are in that country. More generalized wage relations result in higher levels of involvement, broader citizens' rights, and therefore a more legitimate system.

In this era of globalization, the trend towards exclusion from wage relations not only compromises the objective bases of citizenship, but also endangers the legitimacy of and identification with nation-states and jeopardizes the world capitalist system. First we will examine how the logic of increased involvement generates rights and citizenship, as well as legitimacy and identification with a nationally mediated market economy. Later we will look at how globalization generates the internationalization of the labour market based on exclusion, undermining acquired rights and thus objective citizenship. With globalization the reproductive logic of capital and of the labour force are no longer bound by a national context, and as a result citizenship begins to lose its national character. We will then look at different approaches to building a new society involving world citizenship grounded in a solidarity ethic.

The Welfare State and Citizenship Based on Market Relations

Until a few decades ago the nation-state was the referential framework for accumulation. The reproductive logic of capital and the labour

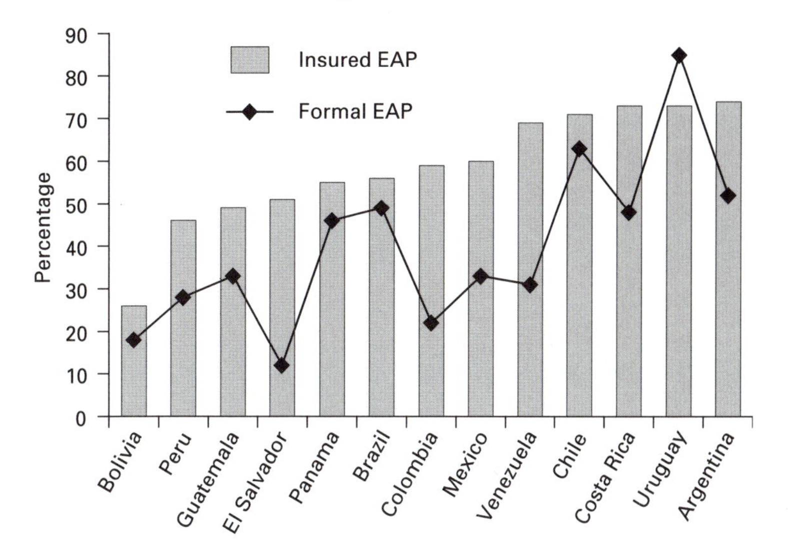

Figure 4.1 Socially insured economically active population in Latin America, 1979–80 (as % of EAP) (*Source*: Isuani, 1986: 119)

force was centred in the nation-state as well. In this context, lower levels of involvement – less widespread wage relations in a given nation – correspond to a more easily replaced labour force, which in turn leads to lower wages and less emphasis on workers' health and social and economic security. Figure 4.1 illustrates the relationship between the prevalence of wage relations and social security coverage in Latin America in 1980.

In peripheral countries with high replacement capacity, the reproduction of workers – as an opposing class to capital – depends on the availability of new workers, even if their biological reproduction as individuals and families is virtually undermined. Despite poverty, malnutrition and lack of health care, capital has constant access to new and generally younger labourers (see Figure 4.2), willing to work in deplorable conditions, who are the product of the dissolution of noncapitalist ties. In other words, the working class is reproduced as a class even when unable to reproduce as individuals.

Employers' flexibility when hiring workers allows them to recruit the most suitable workforce for any amount of time. Men are more likely to be hired than women (see Table 4.1), resulting in greater

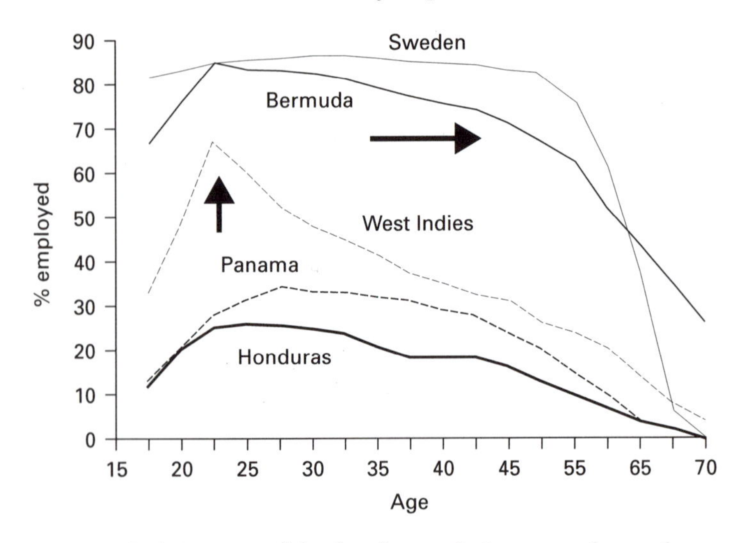

Figure 4.2 Activity rates of the female population as employees, by age, in selected countries, 1980 (*Source*: Dierckxsens, 1990: 28)

economic and social insecurity for women than for men. Their placement chances are much lower, and if they cannot find something themselves they must rely on their partners' highly unstable employment. This is a very dependent and subordinate position.

The working class reproduces as a class to the extent that capital replaces the worn-out labour force – disabled or just too old – with newer, often younger and/or immigrant workers. They are employed under very flexible terms and given the least possible social and economic security (Marshal, 1981: 112; Campanario and Dierckxsens, 1984). Lower economic and social security lead to more radical labour demands, although being easily replaceable also affects their organizational capabilities. Uniting around demands to improve objective working conditions involves organizing, but that requires a certain degree of job stability. Employers can easily replace organized with nonorganized workers – a significant impediment to organization. However, it also leads to more radical questioning of society and the state tends to respond with force. Under conditions of limited involvement the social rights of those directly excluded and of the entire population are reduced to a minimum, as is the regime's legitimacy and citizens' identification with it.

Table 4.1 Male and female wage labour force participation rates, by country, 1980

Selected countries	Salaried workers (%)	Global rate of women's participation in economic activity	No. of active women per 100 active men	Salaried workers in female EAP (%)	No. of male salaried workers for every female salaried worker
Haiti	15.5	36.9	70.8	18.7	1.1
Togo	18.6	28.3	74.3	3.1	5.7
Nigeria	33.7	20.6	47.8	15.7	4.6
Guatemala	43.5	8.1	16.9	66.0	3.9
Honduras	44.0	9.7	20.6	57.8	2.0
Panama	57.3	17.2	37.6	78.3	2.0
El Salvador	63.2	22.7	47.8	56.8	2.2
Costa Rica	67.8	18.9	35.6	89.1	2.7
Barbados	68.7	40.0	77.6	75.5	1.2
Trinidad and Tobago	74.8	37.4	45.8	73.5	2.0
Bermuda	85.7	51.3	78.4	92.8	1.1
United States	88.7	40.3	70.6	92.3	1.2
Sweden	89.3	45.7	79.6	92.9	1.1

Source: Dierckxsens, 1990: 27.

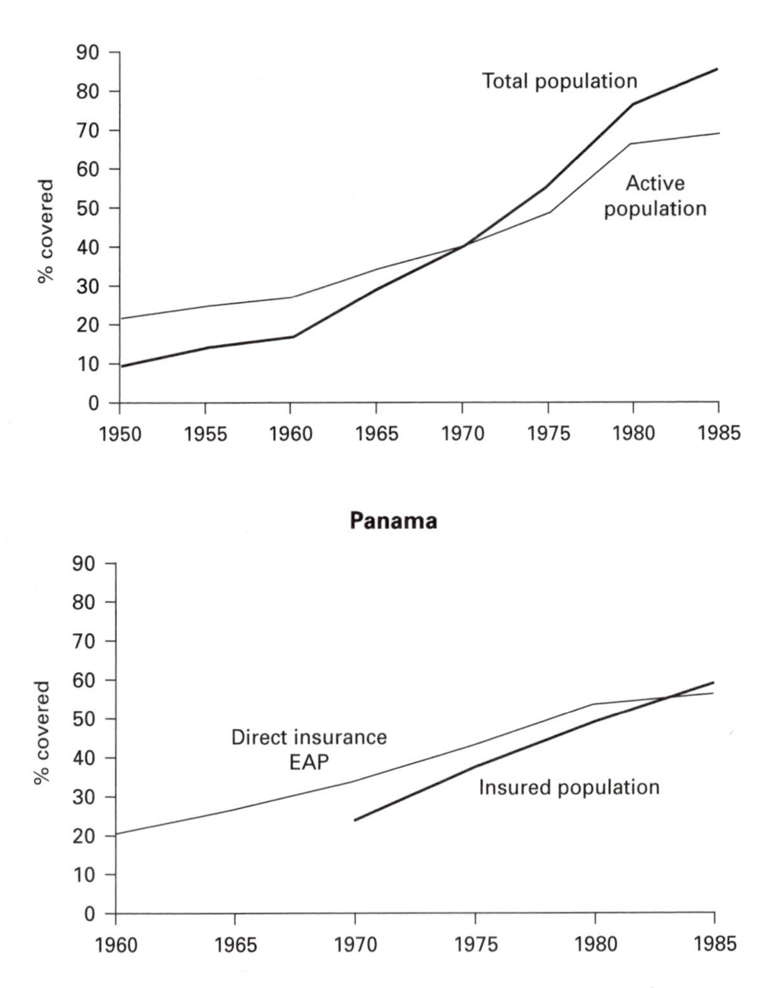

Figure 4.3 Social security coverage in Costa Rica, 1950–85, and Panama, 1960–85 (*Source*: Dierckxsens, 1995: Figures 21 and 22)

The development of the social welfare state contrasts with that of the authoritarian state. Since it is based on the existence of widespread wage relations, the former occurs primarily but not exclusively in major industrialized countries. It results in a less replaceable, more highly skilled workforce that is hired under less flexible conditions and paid higher wages. Greater job stability leads to longer economically active lives for wage labourers and consequently it becomes important to take better care of them.

The conservation and reproduction of workers' labour power is essential to their reproduction as the class in opposition to capital. As future generations of workers are recruited more and more exclusively among workers and their children and less through noncapitalist ties (in retreat), salaries and social security are extended to cover more than just the active population (see Figure 4.3). As wage relations become generalized as the primary labour model, social security is also gradually extended to cover the dependent population (children, housewives).

Human relationships are increasingly monetarized as market relations spread to other spheres including labour. Mutual aid and local solidarity are thus relegated to more restricted spheres of daily life. Solidarity is monetarized and institutionalized through all sorts of social security loans on a national level. Regarding institutional solidarity, employers and employees meet more and more often at the negotiating table and less frequently on the battlefield. Greater job stability and less job flexibility are conducive to worker organization. However, a certain degree of correlation between employers' and workers' interests leads workers to question the system itself less and to become more involved in the debate on national product allocation. Under capitalism organized labour achieved its highest levels of participation in this allocation during the Keynesian period, when full employment was meant to increase global demand. Citizenship and legitimization of the system itself reached their highest expression.

The decreased replaceability that characterized the postwar period led to a greater demand for female and immigrant workers as a means of protecting a degree of contractual flexibility. Migratory movements generally flowed from countries with greater to those with lesser replacement capabilities – from South to North. Since women are more replaceable than are men, they exert more pressure on the labour market. They are more willing to work for lower wages in their own country and abroad, which helps explains their relatively high numbers among immigrants (see Table 4.2).

Compared to men, women's incorporation into the paid labour market is relatively slow, which leads to their being more replaceable than men and receiving lower wages for similar work (see Figure 4.4)

Table 4.2 Emigration of women from Latin America to the USA, 1980

Country	Women per 100 immigrant men (no.)	Active women per 100 active men		Women aged 20 and older, with 12 + years of education (%)
		Immigrants	Non-migrants in countries of origin	
Nicaragua	149	108	–	55
Panama	144	113	47	73
Honduras	139	102	19	53
Costa Rica	135	93	28	60
El Salvador	129	100	54	40
Brazil	125	90	36	70
Paraguay	125	71	25	71
Dominican Republic	124	82	–	31
Guatemala	118	85	17	40
Colombia	116	83	36	61
Cuba	114	80	45	56
Ecuador	113	80	26	56
Bolivia	106	75	31	82
Haiti	106	86	75	63
Peru	104	69	34	75
Chile	103	70	43	75
Uruguay	100	69	50	61
Argentina	98	62	18	71
Venezuela	94	70	38	79
Mexico	90	46	39	23

Source: Dierckxsens, 1990: 133.

and fewer social guarantees, especially in pension plans. In other words, they are second-class citizens because of their vulnerable position in market relations. Ethnic minorities, such as Latin American indigenous communities, fare even worse since their ties to the market are weak or nonexistent.

Until women's involvement became more widespread they were engaged primarily in unpaid domestic labour. Although both are neces-

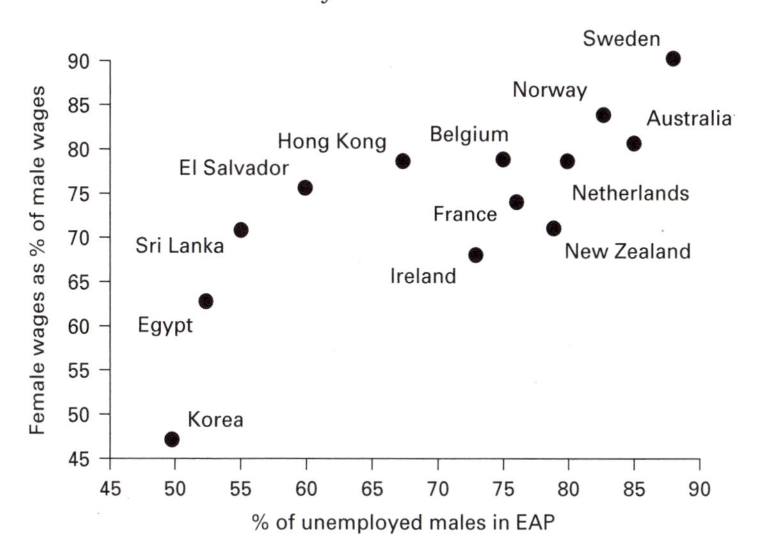

Figure 4.4 Women's salaries as percentage of men's salaries in manufacturing, selected countries, 1980 (*Source*: Dierckxsens, 1990: 108)

sary and complementary aspects of reproduction, paid labour offers more independence for survival while domestic labour is dependent on paid labour. This subordination is institutionalized as women are incorporated into the paid labour market. Women tend to be hired for subordinate positions, reproducing gender supremacy in the structured labour sector (see Table 4.3).

Widespread incorporation of women into the paid labour force, however, has unleashed the struggle for more equitable job allocation,

Table 4.3 Male and female economic participation rates, Costa Rica, 1987

	Women		Men		Women/100 men	
Occupation	Private	State	Private	State	Private	State
Professionals	8.8	48.9	8.8	31.9	47.3	103.3
Managers	0.8	3.3	4.2	6.8	8.8	33.3
Others	90.4	47.8	87.0	61.3	–	–
Total	100	100	100	100	–	–

Source: Dierckxsens, 1990: 125.

income, management positions, and political posts – for equality as citizens. The women's movements for nondiscriminatory citizenship are different in each country, but are not restricted to issues specific to each nation. They transcend national borders, extending the demand for equitable citizenship and solidarity throughout the world.

Globalization of the Labour Market

The accelerated integration of the world market and a flood of foreign direct investment (FDI) have defined the era of globalization. It is not the first time this has occurred in the history of capitalism. From a certain angle, the world economy is less integrated now than it was just before the First World War. Wolf (1997: 14) claims that prior to 1914 British FDI at its peak represented up to 9% of its GDP, twice the amount either Germany or Japan invested abroad in the 1980s. At that time gold was the single currency and there was freer and greater workforce mobility beyond national borders.

Globalization of capital is a product of the nineteenth-century expansion of nation-states based on the territorial division of the world among the major powers of that time. Any later changes would lead to war among these powers as occurred, for example, in the First World War. Expanding domestic markets, employment, social welfare and workers' purchasing power were major concerns following the crisis of the 1930s and especially after the Second World War and in industrialized nations (Barahona, 1997: 4). The nation-state played a major role in this process.

Promotion of the domestic market has given way to a new unbridled dispute over world markets, although it no longer implies territorial occupation. Conflicts between nations have become more economic than before the world wars. Nation-states and domestic markets have played a major role in the post-Second World War era, but the state's role in the global battle for world markets is clearly subordinated to transnational interests. There has been a resurgence of FDI under global *laissez-faire* leading to transnational production of goods and services and a global labour market that is controlled less and less by the laws regulating domestic job markets.

Specifically, labour market globalization brings a shift in the workforce's reproductive logic. Peripheral countries' share of industrial jobs

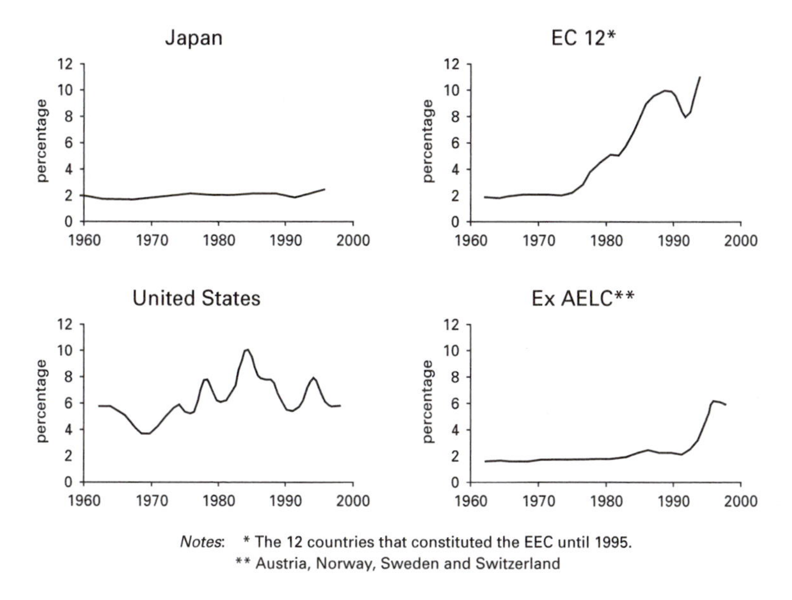

Figure 4.5 Unemployment rates in industrialized countries, 1960–95 (*Source*: OIT, 1996: 54)

has gradually increased from 43% a few decades ago to 53% in 1990 (Freeman, 1994). Donahue (1994) and others are only slightly exaggerating when they state that in order to attract foreign investment 'the world has become a giant bazaar where nations compete against each other to sell their workforce at lower and lower prices'.

More intense competition, along with stagnant economic growth and stronger workforce competition, have led to deterioration of labour conditions in many parts of the world. Since 1973 unemployment rates have risen in most industrialized nations and employment has worsened in developing countries (ILO, 1996: 7). See Figure 4.5.

In 1996:

> unemployment was still high in many industrialized countries ... In July 1996 there was 11.3% unemployment in the European Union, slightly higher than the year before ... Outside of Europe it rose slightly in Australia and Japan to 8.5% and 3.4% respectively. It remained steady at 9.8% in Canada and continued to fall in the US from 5.7% to 5.4%. It remained high at 11.6% or more in transitional economies. (ILO, 1996: XIII).

Table 4.4 Unemployment rates, Latin America, 1975–93

	Growth of active population			Growth of total employment			Total unemployment rate		
	1975–80	1981–85	1986–93	1975–80	1981–85	1986–93	1975–80	1981–85	1986–93
Bolivia	2.13	2.7	2.71	2.68	-0.38	1.97	5.48	13.5	19.5
Brazil	3.37	2.33	2.12	3.94	4.3	2.93			
Chile	2.54	2.58	1.98	3.74	0.95	3.33	12.92	14.3	6.01
Colombia	2.51	2.84	2.42						
Costa Rica	4.03	3.07	2.47	4.01	2.74	3.62	5.22	7.78	4.93
Mexico	4.41	3.23	3.13						
Argentina	0.82	1.1	1.31						
Ecuador	2.79	3.08	2.95						
Honduras	3.47	3.84	3.9						
Panama	2.53	2.96	2.74	3.42	3.79	2.35	7.74	10.13	14.1
Uruguay	0.5	0.64	0.84						
Dominican Republic	3.22	3.46	3.14						
El Salvador	3.02	2.92	3.29						
Guatemala	2.08	2.82	3.16						
Haiti	0.94	1.98	2.15						
Nicaragua	2.7	3.78	3.94					3.2	8.33
Paraguay	3.5	3.13	2.86						
Peru	3.39	2.91	2.83						
Venezuela	4.83	3.48	3.09	3.91	1.81	4.1	5.53	9.92	8.81

Source: ILO, 1996: 158.

Table 4.5 Unemployment rates, by level of skill, 1970–90

		Late 1970s–early 1980s	Late 1980s–early 1990s
West Germany:	Least skilled quartile	3.6	11.0
	Most skilled quartile	1.7	4.2
Australia:	Least skilled quartile	5.8	7.1
	Most skilled quartile	1.9	2.9
Canada:	Least skilled quartile	6.7	9.3
	Most skilled quartile	2.6	3.5
United States:	Least skilled quartile	6.4	8.1
	Most skilled quartile	1.8	2.3
France:	Least skilled quartile	3.9	8.9
	Most skilled quartile	2.6	3.1
Italy:	Least skilled quartile	1.4	4.9
	Most skilled quartile	3.0	4.5
Japan:	Least skilled quartile	2.7	2.9
	Most skilled quartile	1.3	1.1
United Kingdom:	Least skilled quartile	5.9	11.6
	Most skilled quartile	1.9	2.2

Source: ILO, 1996: 59.

In the same report the ILO indicates that unemployment in Latin America remains at around 10%, with no sign of a reversal (see Table 4.4). The situation in Africa is also critical even though 1996 data were unavailable.

In the context of globalization the economic dispute over the world market does not stimulate employment, but neither does it result in the end of labour as some authors have claimed (Rifkin, 1997). Globalization that fails to promote employment results in greater labour flexibility, and lower salaries, and negatively affects labour standards around the world. Workers in national labour markets that are more open to foreign competition are left in weaker bargaining positions (Rodrik, 1997). The threat by transnational corporations to relocate abroad limits a host government's ability to impose taxes on them – which explains the recent fiscal decline – and to enforce labour standards (Martin and Schumann, 1996: 91–5; ILO, 1996: 5), which together accentuate income concentration.

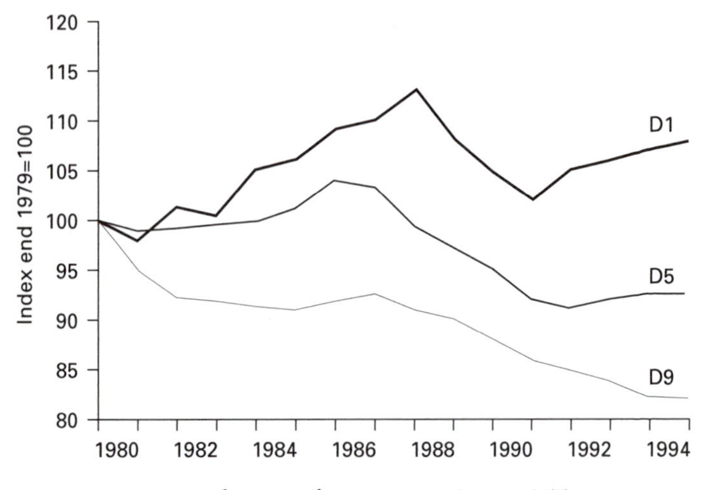

Figure 4.6 Growth in equality, 1979–95 (*Source*: OIT, 1996: 69)

As a result of the labour market's growing integration around the world, reproduction of the workforce takes place less and less in the national arena. This is especially true for workers in less skilled and more routine jobs, which are also predominant in those activities attracting most FDI in the periphery. As a result these workers are more and more replaceable throughout the world and the gap between unemployment rates for skilled and unskilled workers is growing, as illustrated in Table 4.5.

This leads to declining salaries for unskilled and highly routine jobs in core countries, as has been the case in the USA (see Figure 4.6). Foreign capital investments in the periphery do not bring higher salaries to those countries. In practice, less competitive local industry is destroyed and labour markets deteriorate as the markets are overrun with transnational goods. Underemployment and unemployment remain high and the replaceability of labour in these countries allows very competitive salaries from the employers' point of view.

The more aggressively a country uses labour flexibility in order to adjust to international salary levels, the greater the impact on salaries even though unemployment may not decline. Labour flexibility applies especially to unskilled and/or highly routine jobs that are internationally more replaceable, and therefore primarily affect the lowest salaries.

Table 4.6 Global inequality: the growing income gap, 1960–89

	Poorest 20%	Wealthiest 20%	Relation of wealthy to poor	Gini coefficient
1960	2.3	70.2	30 to 1	0.69
1970	2.3	73.9	32 to 1	0.71
1980	1.7	76.3	45 to 1	0.79
1989	1.4	82.7	59 to 1	0.87

Source: UNDP, 1992: 36.

This results in a wide income gap (see Table 4.6) and a growing number of workers with below poverty-level incomes (ILO, 1996: 70–5).

The World Economy, Division of Labour and Citizenship

With globalization, labour relations and economic appropriation processes and structures have spread throughout the world, spanning territories and borders, nations and nationalities, and subordinating nation-states to the new economic powers. Scholars still commonly use the nation-state perspective to interpret the global society. Authors such as Wallerstein (1991) still see a world economy structured around nation-states. He recognizes the importance of transnational corporations but reaffirms that of sovereign nation-states, even though it is limited by their interdependence and the power of stronger states over others.

Octavio Ianni (1996: 21–7) takes this somewhat traditional perspective a step further, indicating that nation-state sovereignty is not just limited but is completely undermined: 'Clearly neither the concept of sovereignty nor the nation-state disappear but they are radically undermined ... Although ... the sovereign nation-state remains or is even recreated, it is changing shape as regards the configuration and movements of global society.'

Wallerstein (1991) and Braudel (1991: 41–78) are primarily concerned with more conventional integration issues, whether economic, geographical or historical. For Wallerstein the world economy becomes universal in that it includes all national states to some degree, and this in turn determines whether they are part of the core or the periphery (Camilleri, 1992: 77, in Ianni: 1996). Both Wallerstein and Braudel explain the globalization process, but they portray the nation-state as an agent that undergoes no essential transformations. It is clearly a historical reality, a process, but their analyses are limited by this purely national approach. Braudel is intrigued with trying to determine France's position in the world, while Wallerstein seeks to unlock the secret of US capitalist supremacy (Ianni, 1996: 25).

From a different perspective, authors such as Samir Amin and Gunder Frank recognize that TNCs traverse national borders, creating new challenges for governments and demonstrating that the notions of national sovereignty, imperialism and dependency do not reflect current realities. However, both authors continue to use a nation-state approach in their analyses of global society. They become inspired by the idea that national projects or national liberation movements can lead to a people's emancipation. Ianni (1996: 26) responds that it is not a matter of denying local, national, regional or global manifestations of reality. He uses the historicity of nation-states and the appearance of new, more powerful centres of world power, sovereignty and hegemony to detect major historical ruptures around the world.

Robert Reich, author of *The Work of Nations* and secretary of labor during the first Clinton administration, points out that the economy has spanned national borders but labour has not. He claims that in the twenty-first century there will be no national products or technology, and only the population residing within a country's borders will belong to it. A nation's main political mission will be to keep and attract a skilled labour force rather than to manage economic forces in order to hold onto national investments and attract foreign ones (Reich, 1993: 13). TNCs no longer subordinate their stockholders' interests to those of their home nation. Capitalism is inescapably organized around profits and not patriotism. Executive officers do not waver when profitability demands that production relocate from a national factory to one abroad (ibid.: 142). He predicts that soon no one will demand protection for US national industry from the lower wages paid by foreign competitors (ibid.: 275).

Reich understands that nation-states do not control transnational capital – quite the opposite. Instead it serves the interests of borderless private states. National policies cannot be designed around investments, since these no longer serve national interests. Labour policies, however, offer an alternative scenario. Protection of national investment in industrial sectors with highly routine jobs is detrimental for the nation. Protecting these national investments – textile or automotive industries – means defending shrinking salaries. Whether foreign or domestic, the investments that must be attracted and retained are those that provide jobs for skilled labour.

Reich claims that their foreign direct investments are transforming TNCs into world networks. Zero-sum nationalism – either our companies or theirs win – feeds a sort of paranoia that avoids reality and only promotes stagnation. He proposes an alternative, more cosmopolitan vision. The economic welfare of a country – specifically the USA – depends no longer on its companies' profitability or its industries' drive at home or abroad, but rather on the value added by labour inside the country regardless of investment sources (ibid.: 296). These economic policies allow and even promote the relocation of domestic companies with predominantly low-skilled labour to less developed nations while seeking to attract, retain and develop both foreign and domestic ones with highly skilled labour. According to this new strategy, wealth is obtained through skilled non-routine labour within a given nation, regardless of the source of the investment.

Ultimately Reich is bound by the traditional nation-state perspective. His primary concern is to determine how the USA can maintain hegemony using skilled labour regardless of transnational capital shifts. A nation-state's economic policies based on domestic ownership of investments must be replaced with others based on the concentration of skilled labour in the country. This explains how Reich can be so accepting, for example, of British ownership of such a typically US company as Burger King and of strong US participation (40–50%) in such typically foreign companies as Isuzu, Daewoo and Saab (ibid.: 131, 310). He claims that the future welfare of the USA depends not on the nationality of investments *per se* but on economic policies that manage to attract, retain and develop profitable activities or link cutting-edge workers with transnationals. In other words, borderless private states must concentrate their most dynamic and high return investments in the USA.

From this perspective, cutting-edge workers add more value to national wealth than do workers in more routine jobs. Reich calls these cutting-edge workers – such as experts in strategic negotiations and problem identification and resolution – symbolic-analytical servants. They are strongly tied to international capital wherever it may be. These activities often take place many thousands of kilometres apart providing there is telephone, fax and modem services and a nearby international airport. Reich takes his proposals a step further: even if the investments are abroad, these workers must be located in the USA. He proudly calls attention to the growing army of lawyers, financial consultants and intermediaries in the United States who add more value and contribute more to national wealth than other types of workers (ibid.: 190). In its search for higher than average profits, transnational capital's shift towards nonproductive sectors in general, and especially finance, leads to highly nonproductive jobs with well above average pay.

These economic policies result in the concentration of these highly skilled and nonproductive but well-paid jobs in core countries and of productive capital and medium- and low-skilled more routine jobs in the periphery. The class structure around the world is transformed, geographically concentrating cutting-edge workers in core countries, while the productive base is increasingly located in the periphery. Just as the gap between the wealthy and the poor within a nation will continue to widen as workers in routine jobs become more replaceable, so too the distance widens between wealthy and less advanced nations, where routine jobs are increasingly concentrated. In brief, these are exclusionary economic policies on a global scale.

This growing replaceability leads to the loss of hard-won rights and citizenship. Rising unemployment and/or the replaceability of the workforce results in greater job instability, pressure to lower real wages and difficulties for maintaining social rights acquired in times of greater stability. In other words, there is growing pressure to dismantle the social welfare state as the workforce becomes more replaceable.

In the 1970s replaceability was still dropping in core countries and the social welfare state and citizenship were being strengthened. These nations were an example for a periphery that had higher replaceability and thus less developed social rights and citizenship. Increased replaceability in core nations has led to the erosion of hard-won social rights and a loss of citizenship, while peripheral countries set the example for them in this respect.

Following this logic, citizenship in a market economy clearly entails participation in those market relations. Increasing exclusion leads to disenfranchisement and loss of social rights for those directly affected as well as for the highly replaceable population that is not yet affected. Greater exclusion means fewer rights and its extreme expression would be the very loss of the right to life (Forrester, 1997).

New Goals for the Global Economy: An Alternative Perspective

As a result of labour market globalization, workforce replacement is no longer restricted to the context of single nation-states. This is especially true for unskilled labour but has gradually also affected skilled labour as well. From the global perspective of transnational capital the working class reproduces as such on a more global level and less on a national level. Greater flexibility of labour relations merely indicates increasing replaceability along with falling wages and social conditions, leading to greater labour exploitation.

Increased replaceability leads to a breakdown of the social contract and the disintegration of the labour unions and institutional solidarity that characterize the social welfare state. At the same time local solidarity and mutual aid have reached all-time lows as most aspects of daily life have become monetarized.

Greater exclusion in most of the world has led trade unions to become gradually weaker. Nation-states' fears that investments may decide to relocate lead them to meet TNC demands and distance themselves from unions, thus breaking the existing tripartite social contract. Workers are more on the defensive and are less involved in the administration and allocation of the national product. Society is being split even in Latin America, where non-salaried workers are an important sector of the working class. Unemployment and underemployment, along with the rise of informal labour, are symptoms of growing labour instability that hinders the development of collective actors (Ezcurra, 1997: 27).

From a broader perspective, labour unions' retreat in many countries can be seen as the turning point towards a new organizational era. Just as the workforce is currently reproduced more on a global than on a national scale, the scope of their organizations must also span national borders. The old system of unionizing by company and sector in a given country is over. As Lula-da Silva indicated (1997) the focus of union organizing has increasingly shifted to TNCs. This will become a significant international trend, as has already occurred in Latin America.

The article 'Workers of the World, UNITE' published in *North American Council on Latin America* (May/June 1997: 5) claims that for every Mexican, Central American and Caribbean migrant to the USA another is hired by a US maquila in these Southern nations. There they find a cheaper workforce, lower taxes and more relaxed social and ecological regulations than at home, as well as trade agreements giving them the same access to US markets as any other in that country. Unfortunately for these companies, trade unions in the North and South have recently begun to join forces. The Union of Needle-traders and Textile Employees of the USA has joined with its Southern counterparts and in March 1997 they met to plan future joint actions.

Lula-da Silva, the well-known Brazilian labour leader and former presidential candidate, claims that labour unions need to shift their focus: 'The labor movement's discourse and practice must evolve to adapt to the current situation and participate in decision-making. They must become *citizen unions* that are *less corporate and more open*' (Lula-da Silva, 1997: 18, emphasis added).

In the same article he points out that Volkswagen, for example, does not answer to either the German or Brazilian governments regarding its investments, and much less to their citizens. Thus the only alternative is to use political pressure to create conditions in these two countries that would bring this transnational corporation to the bargaining table to discuss issues other than just profits. He concludes that the new dynamic of the world economy's productive sector fosters unification of the labour movement.

In other words, trade unions are not dead. The conditions are ripe for citizens around the world to join together and demand accountability from TNCs. This movement has great potential for growth outside official political circles if it can join with other citizens' organizations in a single, less corporate and broader, global movement united around TNC-centred demands.

More and more frequently citizen groups are denouncing abuses by specific TNCs on ethical grounds. Such demands would have been impossible during the Cold War since they would have been branded communist, but now ethical issues can rally the great masses. Concrete opposition to child labour and forced labour, for example, has driven Shell – one of the world's largest TNCs – to formulate a code of conduct to be followed by the entire corporation. This represents an important step towards accountability to citizens.

The World Citizens' Movement has begun to denounce abuses such as child and forced labour by TNC subsidiaries around the world, similar to those in early nineteenth-century England, and has gradually broadened its scope to include other issues, such as consumers' and workers' health. Health problems caused by certain products have become a major issue confronting TNCs, and consumer boycotts against their import and consumption have become more frequent. Human rights organizations have added their voices to demands that TNCs be made accountable for the health problems suffered by workers and consumers as a result of their products or input materials – for example, the accusations and claims made by South and Central American human rights organizations of worker sterilization by US banana companies. Recent demands and lawsuits against US tobacco companies for smoking-related health problems are another case in point.

Joint actions by labour unions, consumer groups and human rights organizations represent the sectorial expression of these demands for TNC accountability to the world's citizens. These activities can be developed simultaneously on the local, national and global levels, which in turn represent their geographical expression. The combination and coordination of these two leads to the consolidation of a world citizenry engaged in challenging TNCs and neoliberalism in general.

It is crucial that organizations focus on TNC-related issues, but challenging these corporations and their neoliberal ideology is equally important. Since globalization encompasses the entire world, any proposal for a more just society must be universal (Ezcurra, 1997: 14). It involves the needs of collective subjects on a global scale who are organized around broad agendas that question neoliberalism's hegemony on ethical grounds. The ecological and women's movements, with their global agendas challenging the concepts of wealth and productive labour, are at the vanguard of collective subjects confronting neoliberal ideology.

The fight against neoliberalism entails constructing a collective social, moral and ethical subject with a spirit of solidarity (Mier, 1997: 51). The notion of the subject confirms that being the master of one's own process and destiny is an integral part of human dignity. The individual subject with freedom – the ability to choose from among diverse finite goods – and consciousness – the ability to discover and value the means for achieving a goal – has been developed in Western society with an individualist and elitist bias that is further accentuated by neoliberalism. It can be countered, however, by social subjects with a spirit of solidarity – moral social subjects whose lives inspire and influence the development of authentic values that are needed to build a society with room for all. Ethical subjects using appropriate reasoning and arguments are able to construct such a society (ibid.: 52s).

Neoliberalism's destructive logic represents an ethic of human sacrifice and is opposed by the logic of the Common Good's reproductive vitality. To opt for the vitality of the whole in function of the Common Good entails creating new values as well as new ethical valuations (González Butrón, 1997: 4). Devising a fair human-centred economic ethic that focuses on decision-making rather than capital and profits is a major challenge in this context. Worldwide solidarity is crucial in order to challenge this economic rationality and must necessarily include the needs and demands of everyone (ibid.: 6).

5

Globalization: The Origin of Private States without Citizens

The Logic of Capital in a No-growth Economy

With the current economic slump it has become even more apparent that competition and the pursuit of profit are the real driving forces of the economy. Competition is defended, promoted and even sold. While it has always been the true motor of the modern economy, its face remained hidden behind the economic growth motive. After the latter lost its status as the motor of economic activity the concentration of wealth has become the last remaining source of profits. And so globalization has also brought economic exclusion and poverty.

Privatization of state-owned businesses, the dismantling of social welfare programmes, and income concentration have increasingly become the major conditions for maintaining profits. Transnational capital's struggle for survival has turned into a fight to the death and made it the sole regulator of the economy. If the Cold War provided a favourable climate for negotiations, its conclusion has underscored absolute faith in the market. An 'unbridled economic world war' has broken out, to use Petrella's expression (1996: 10). This rampant dispute unfolds in the context of slow growth and falling average profit rates and has focused on strengthening market positions. The strategy involves acquiring a greater share of existing wealth instead of promoting growth through investments in new areas to create wealth.

Petrella points out that survival in this new cut-throat competition depends on a TNC's competitive logic. In the North it is argued that without TNC competition there would be no way out of this conflict, or any social or economic welfare and growth in the host country – there would be no salvation. This serves to justify a capitalism that ignores social welfare. Competitiveness is key to winning the battle for markets, but it in turn depends on technological development. Because of the great faith placed in the tools of the system, everyone's salvation lies outside a society. The cult of competitiveness thus results in another cult – technological innovation at the expense of jobs, social welfare programmes, income, hard-won social benefits and the incorporation of women.

The Subordination of Social and Labour Issues to Transnational Interests

Transnational corporations demand direct government support to help them survive this fierce contest. They need public authorities to protect them at home and guarantee them a competitive edge. They contribute heavily to technological research and development programmes at the expense of programmes involving such things as unemployment insurance and social welfare. Only TNCs are considered capable of developing that competitive edge needed to survive this contest and actually able to win (ibid.). Large TNCs have become a force that dictates the rules of the game and the social values in society. Even in more advanced countries, national independence ultimately depends on the survival of their TNCs in cut-throat global competition. The national state is thus subordinate to the TNCs' interests, which paradoxically results in a state that is both more circumscribed and authoritarian and in the simultaneous loss of citizenry.

This competitive obsession fosters investments that strengthen market positions (acquisitions, sophisticated technology, marketing, and other business costs). This cut-throat competition in the globalized market does not lead to economic growth, but instead strengthens certain zones within the wealthiest nations where successful TNCs operate. At the same time, however, this trend leads to increasing differentiation and exclusion in other zones of these nations, not to mention the levels of exclusion reached in the periphery, which includes entire subcontinents. This exclusionary process is advancing like a desert across the globe.

The blind struggle for survival leads capital to focus on research and development in order to improve technology and overtake its rivals, and on investment for acquisition or preservation of existing markets. This curbs economic growth and results in a relative and absolute loss of employment opportunities. According to Petrella (ibid.), even in the most advanced countries, without these technological innovations there can be no national self-determination, nor jobs and economic and social well-being for its people. To avoid national capital's subordination to technologically more advanced foreign capital it must take precedence over everything else.

According to this perspective, the general employment situation depends on TNC competitiveness. Demand for full employment in this context is no longer the guiding factor it was under Keynesianism, since that would endanger the general employment situation. The priority is to safeguard it even though this may lead to increasing structural unemployment, and less stable, lower-paying jobs. Human sacrifices in the form of unemployment, social and economic insecurity and the loss of hard-won benefits are tributes paid in the name of supreme competition.

The working class is asked to sacrifice its economic and social rights to ensure the nation's competitive edge in the global market. Transnational capital's struggle for greater participation leads to greater exclusion of the working class. The economically active population's jobs are threatened by growing numbers of unemployed and their impact on the labour market. The employed feel threatened, and project responsibility for their social and economic insecurities onto the jobless that endanger the system. This cultivates social hatreds and xenophobia, rather than tolerance and solidarity, both within and among nations.

Cycles of Intervention and Deregulation, and the Historical Role of the Nation-state

Hinkelammert (1995: 213–24) has pointed out that the market becomes all-encompassing when competitiveness is a central value in society, in the name of subjects who maximize profits with no mediation and whose end result is efficiency. When this occurs on a worldwide scale it is called globalization. Following Adam Smith and liberal economic thought, the pursuit of individual profit promotes national economic growth. Liberal thought claims that the existence of self-regulatory mechanisms operating by way of the 'invisible hand' ensures that divisive actions are part of the whole that is balanced by the market. Adam Smith claims that actors are unaware of the results of their divisive actions because of that invisible hand, but behave as though they were. This understanding does not disappear. It is shifted from the actors to a structure operating as though it had that understanding. It is transformed into something magical.

Faith in the invisible hand has existed since Adam Smith's time, but cyclically it is taken to greater extremes followed by periods of increasingly stronger intervention. The crisis of the 1830s with its characteristic Manchesterianism resulted in the first-ever development of an entrepreneurial ideology (Hinkelammert, 1984: 81). Extreme *laissez faire* protects business's profits at the expense of a concentration of wealth that in the long run leads to the intensification of the crisis. The crisis of the 1870s and 1880s was followed by a period of government intervention to regulate the invisible hand and develop conscious regulatory policies. Bismarck initiated the social welfare state with its strong emphasis on social security. It was originally meant to assist the less replaceable, primarily middle-class, salaried workforce, but coverage was gradually broadened until the First World War in the more advanced countries. By 1915, 66% of Great Britain's economically active population (EAP) was covered by health insurance, with 70% in Denmark, 43% in Germany and 35% in Norway, but only 15% in the more backward France (Alber, 1982: 236).

Plummeting average profit rates after the First World War brought a broader and renewed faith in *laissez faire* and the total market, eventually leading to the global depression of the 1930s. 'The violence of competition in the world market triggered the economic crisis of 1929–1932' (Gombeaud and Décaillot, 1997: 205). The Great Depression and the protectionism that followed resulted in an extreme form of nationalism that ultimately led to the Second World War. That conflict spawned the conviction that solidarity was needed for a new era of increased state intervention that would include the entire population of industrialized nations and whose most visible expression was the newly universal social security coverage. This was not limited to industrialized nations. Significantly, it also occurred in the more economically developed Southern Cone countries of Latin America, where workforce replaceability had dropped dramatically. Participation in other parts of the region had been extended primarily to the middle class, while the great majority of people were very replaceable and remained excluded (Isuani, 1986: 114, and Mesa-Lago, 1990: 30–1). The postwar Keynesian revolution represented the most developed conscious ideological expression that placed a 'visible hand' – in the form of the social welfare state – to counterbalance the invisible one that had led the economy into a global crisis.

The state took on a much more significant role and by the early 1970s government spending in OECD countries represented about 50% of their GDP. In all these countries – with the crucial exception of the USA – it was almost entirely financed by higher taxes rather than by secular growth of government debt. High profit rates and strong economic growth allowed this high public spending without significantly increasing the public debt until the 1970s (Gough, 1978: 234–40).

The world economic crisis that began in the 1970s is primarily characterized by an absolute drop in economic growth and thus in profit rates. It originated in growing nonproductive investment rather than in rising government spending. The role of the state in the 1970s reflects this crisis. The solution to the crisis for the business class, and for the state representing its interests, could have been found through increased government intervention as a sort of visible hand limiting the invisible one in its search for lucrative nonproductive investment. In the early days of this crisis there was greater government intervention in unemployment matters – though not in the investment trends that caused them. Unemployment led to significant increases in social spending to be financed by a domestic product that had stagnated due to less productive investment. The growing cost of government intervention and the continuing rise of unemployment meant that capital was abstaining from profits that could be made from lower wages resulting from greater pressures in the labour market. Rising unemployment led to falling wages in this context of *laissez faire* policies as long as the government did not interfere. Increased government intervention to deal with the employment situation would mean that capital must give up the immediate higher profit rates as well as the essence of the mode of production itself. It was a choice between imposing tighter restrictions on the invisible hand or giving it much freer rein. The former would have led to the gradual replacement of the invisible hand by a visible one and ultimately of the economic rationality behind the relations of production as well. This would have been an excellent step towards greater humanism. The latter resulted in capital's recalcitrant reaction as it sought its *raison d'être* even at the expense of humankind's well-being.

Rising unemployment in the 1970s led to expansion of the social welfare state in the early days of the crisis, especially in Europe, in the hope of soon finding a way out of the recession. However, investment continued to shift towards nonproductive spheres by-their-content, growth remained sluggish, and social spending became an important factor in the rising fiscal deficit. This deficit came under closer scrutiny during the 1980s from big capital that argued that rising structural unemployment eliminated prospects of economic growth, in other words of increasing profits. Big capital's victory in this battle to raise profits also resulted in the decline of the social welfare state. In the 1990s there has been greater consensus regarding the need to dismantle economic and social welfare programmes.

High structural unemployment means that the workforce can be more easily replaced. It would be easier still without the regulations limiting labour mobility that are included in social contracts established at a time of lower workforce replaceability. It would be much greater if market forces were given free rein. This leads big capital to demand more flexibility in hiring and firing workers, in wages and granting social benefits (Heise, 1996: 21). This represents an increase in profit rates at the expense of direct and indirect wages and is a prime example of the neoliberal maxim of more market and less government.

In a world where growth is extremely sluggish, the drive for profit maximization leads to greater concentration of incomes. The redistribution of wealth includes declining direct and indirect wages and the privatization of government activities in general, including social welfare programmes. Drucker (1994: 84–7) points out that pension funds built up over decades had become a major source of financial capital. In government hands this brought increasing socialization of property. Neoliberals argued, however, that under state control these activities do not produce private profits without costs and thus they are sterile. Under private ownership they would reach maximum efficiency – maximum utility – resulting in progress. The total market is portrayed as the only efficient alternative, promoting privatization especially in the social arena.

Some state-owned companies, such as airlines and telecommunications, for example, would have had a difficult time if they had been developed instead by individual private capital, but they are now a source of potential monopoly profits for private capital. Under government ownership administration of these activities can be more efficient in technical and managerial terms. There are no objections when private capital obtains high profits in its own spheres, but that changes as economic growth slows and average profit rates plummet. From the perspective of private capital these companies use the free market to produce huge private profits. Public debt is regarded as proof of government inefficiency and is often used to acquire state-owned businesses at bargain-basement prices along with the rights to future profits. It is argued that this leads to greater efficiency of the economy in general, but the mere transfer of property does not generate wealth – it is only redistributed. Privatization does not produce economic growth or social well-being, but it does promote the concentration of wealth in the hands of fewer transnational corporations.

Transnational companies are becoming planetary consortia without geographical borders and are gaining increasing power over nation-states, imposing their own interests and thus establishing hegemony. These new sovereign 'private states' are not held accountable for anything to anyone. They are 'private states without citizens' with the power to subordinate numerous national states. In their mortal contest for markets they do not give a second thought to sacrificing natural and human resources on a historically unprecedented scale (Goldsmith, April 1996: 19).

The Limits of Citizenship in the Context of a Capitalism without Borders

In a market economy citizenship depends objectively on people's involvement or lack of involvement in market relations, which also determines their sense of identity as citizens of the society in which they live. This citizenry and their identity develop and change as society itself changes. Global integration of the market and its transformation as the unconditional alternative to the social welfare state and as history's total solution lead to the development of a citizenry without government involvement depending exclusively on market relations. These market relations are now the primary regulators of civil society.

In the subjective sense as citizens' identification with a given society, citizenship becomes rather abstract since it requires the identification with and allegiance to this abstract market. According to authors such as Huber (1994: 177–81), this citizenship or identification with the total market-based society emerges spontaneously as the social welfare state's power erodes. I would argue, however, that neoliberalism leads to a loss of citizenship in both objective and subjective terms. A brief historical examination of citizenship will help explain this trend.

Government intervention was very limited throughout most of the nineteenth century. The market did not yet control most aspects of life and social relations were not as permeated by the market or, consequently, individualism. Solidarity and mutual aid that had originated in nonmercantile economies coexisted with the market. Extraeconomic relations predominated in society. Control of raw materials markets, for example, depended largely on relations of military power. Possession, acquisition and defence of raw materials often entailed physical territorial occupation and colonization. The type of allegiance to a given society and state expected from citizens was primarily extra-economic, as best expressed in the often compulsory conscription for territorial defence and occupation. Those draftees were marginalized from market relations, in other words, objectively they were not even citizens, and there was minimum expression of their identification with the society for which they were fighting.

The Bismarck era and especially Keynesian social welfare states led to the monetization and institutionalization of mutual aid-based solidarity through government intervention in social welfare. Citizens' allegiance to the state became monetary, and its commitment to them was institutionalized and also assumed a monetary expression. Citizenship thus became the identification with the social contracts between capitalists, workers and the government and with their often monetary rights and responsibilities.

During the neoliberal period citizenship took on a more abstract and alienating expression of the dominant system's history. Increasing exclusion was accompanied by a loss of rights and thus of citizenship. Solidarity and mutual aid for concrete persons became a thing of the past. Institutional solidarity and government-controlled social welfare programmes deteriorated and the market increasingly regulated relations. In subjective terms, citizenship came to mean people's identification with the same market that was slashing their rights along with objective citizenship. This resulted in an alienating commitment to the market and to an abstract society threatening to exclude them.

The nineteenth-century notion of citizens as alienated subjects of a specific nation has given way to one of alienated subjects of a borderless invisible market. Being a citizen no longer means identifying with and implementing a social contract established with state and employer involvement and obligations. It now entails commitment to an abstract market whose rules exclude citizens (Drucker, 1994: 183–9; Gough, 1978: 53–92). In this case, justice involves enforcing the laws of the market (Hayek, 1992: 56).

The new alienated citizen – personified as the *homo oeconomicus* who carefully calculates all choices – has become humankind's 'natural state'. Due to this perspective's hegemony this abstract 'human nature' has come to be accepted as universal, as present in all societies in every period of time and in all fields or aspects of life. These economists believe they have discovered a fundamental truth about human nature. Becker (cited by Huber, 1994) is an unfortunate representative of this trend who went so far as to incorporate racism into this logic. The neoclassical assumption that personal material interests are given top priority by all human beings over and above all else is a false and purely ideological notion that actually contradicts human nature. Virtues such as solidarity, empathy, honesty, brotherhood, trust and loyalty are not derived from the theory of rational decisions made by the so-called *homo oeconomicus*. Commitment and identification with society – the subjective citizen – do not arise from rational means–ends decisions, but actually destroy them. Neoliberalism spells the end of citizenship. Huber's claim (1994: 177–81) that identification with a total market-based society arises spontaneously from the remains of a crumbling social welfare state is pure ideology.

Totalization of the market and its cut-throat competition tend to asphyxiate values such as solidarity, loyality and trust in a society. Mounting concentration of wealth, exclusion, the cynical contempt of the disenfranchised, etc. result in a loss of solidarity and thus escalate the violence and false expenditures (*faux frais*) that curb a society's growth and well-being. The widespread emergence of private security forces, the growing army of lawyers and long lines to get into over-populated prisons are testimony to the lack of identification with society. An authoritarian, repressive state is the logical consequence. Values of solidarity have lost more ground and the false costs incurred in maintaining the 'New Order' are higher where neoliberalism is more developed (Fukuyama, 1995: 360).

The Limits of Capitalism without Citizens

The market economy's efficiency depends on competitiveness which, in turn, is driven by investments in key sectors, including continuous technological development. Capital focuses on technology in this battle. Sluggish growth prompts more aggressive defence of market positions and total faith in the tools for capital's survival as such. When the economy has slowed to a near standstill this trend of more aggressive technological development results in greater exclusion of workers. At times of significant expansion the replacement of jobs by technology is compensated by the development of new economic activities. On the other hand, slow growth leads to more aggressive competition and stimulates two-way exclusion.

By idealizing technology as a competitive and productive force we tend to overlook others that are strongly rooted in non-market social relations. Fukuyama (1995) shows that differing growth rates in East and West cannot be seen as mere technological differences that tend to balance out. Instead they are due in large part to the different types of citizenry and civil society found in the East. The notion of a total market disregards this fundamental aspect of human beings: identification with a given society, loyalty and the ability to trust others (Drucker, 1994: 169). The development of the total market reveals the limits of *homo oeconomicus'* efficiency as technology's competitive edge tends to even out and citizens begin to gain an upper hand.

In the past the most successful competitors were those who invented new products. Today, however, the competitive edge comes more from new technological processes for the same products than from research and development of new ones. It has become much cheaper to reproduce existing products with new processes and much more expensive to develop new ones. Perfecting processes or applying them to different areas requires less investment (in research and development) than creating truly new products. Those who can make a product more cheaply using a new process can take control of it away from the original inventor (Thurow, 1992: 52–4). As a result, technological differences among major world competitors – Europe, the USA and Japan – continue to shrink.

There is another argument that reduces the progressive strength of technology investments. Transnational corporations' battle for markets transcends national borders and as a result less technological development is achieved through greenfield investments and more through acquisitions. This has led to competition among 'consortia without borders or citizens' whose economic arenas are not limited by national borders. The economic blocs are characterized by an intermediate stage in transnational capital's efforts to overcome the limits imposed by all types of borders. Identification with a community beyond the confines of the national state, in other words with a more global citizenry, has not been advanced in the same direction and globalization has not included such a project. The European Union has made the most progress towards integration and has established the free circulation of capital (1990), the creation of a single market (1992) and a single currency (1999) as top priorities. However, there is no plan to create a single citizenry (Julien, 1996). On the contrary, amid economic integration there is a tendency towards separatism: Scotland, Flanders, the Basque country, and Corsica among others.

Development of the unified market has broadened the field for transnational capital and at the same time weakened citizens and their identification with this new economic arena. Neoliberals believed that a citizenry would emerge spontaneously. Instead regionalization's impact on citizens has included significant concentration of capital while excluding sectors, geographical regions and even entire countries. This has resulted in greater identification with a more concrete community that is closer, often much older and with a greater sense of right to life, in spite of its much smaller territory, rather than with this increasingly abstract market that is gradually excluding them. Paradoxically, economic globalization and the simultaneous integration of economic blocs have led to separatism on linguistic, ethnic, cultural and other extraeconomic bases (Goldsmith, 1996: 18–19).

From the perspective of economic rationality, this separatism has been classified as tribalism (Drucker, 1994: 167–9). Identification develops with a real, concrete community, however, and not in the abstract. Historically nation-states emerged with the often coercive integration of culturally diverse peoples. The total market tends to mould human beings into *homo oeconomicus* that belong to an increasingly abstract society – a global village – with fewer and fewer ties to any nation-state. To avoid losing their identity human beings seek 'irrational ties' with a closer and more concrete community where they feel their rights are more protected and with which they thus identify more fully. Decreasing identification with nation-states has resulted in localism and separatism rather than in the creation of a more global citizenry.

Neomercantilists such as James Fallows (1993), Clyde Prestowitz (1988) and Laura Tyson (1993) claim that the dynamic East Asian economies were successful because they did *not* follow the rules of the free market. Substantial state intervention in the economy (for productive sectors) and citizens' strong identification with their nation gave the East a competitive edge over the West, causing considerable concern in the latter region. The survival of premodern values in the East, such as the prevalence of an individual's responsibilities to the community over individual rights, unifies a society more than the atomizing individualism that has developed out of centuries of Western market economy. Identification with the nation in the East is a legacy of precapitalist relations of production that provide a competitive edge while they last. This citizenship, identification, commitment and loyalty to the community has been lost in the West. Drucker (1994: 169–71) claims that this citizenship will *not* re-emerge spontaneously in the West with the disappearance of centralized state power, but he affirms that salvaging it is an important new task.

Social services must be developed and civil society restored. Drucker (1994: 189–94) argues that postcapitalist society requires a citizenry that is not based on the allegiance or identification of its constituents and should not be organized on the basis of proximity and segregation, but this citizenry is not cultivated in the framework of market relations. Identification with the community and a spirit of community in the West have only developed outside these market relations. Identification with the community survives in unpaid volunteer labour and nonprofit organizations. One works out of a sense of commitment and identification as a volunteer or without pay. This is irrational from the perspective of *homo oeconomicus* even when it provides a motivation for labour.

Drucker goes on to show that all Western countries must stimulate this autonomous social sector of volunteer community organizations in order to restore civil society. Postcapitalist society depends on this 'citizen greenhouse' for this, since it cannot generate such irrationality within its system. Historically capitalism has fed from noncapitalist relations like a vampire and when postcapitalist society finds them missing it feels the need to re-create them for its own survival but is actually unable to do so. Recent decentralization policies that have shifted power to municipalities along with funds from nonprofit and nongovernmental organizations (NGOs) must be seen in this light. Historically many of these NGOs were founded on the basis of commitments to specific communities. Promoting funding for civil society and for restoring its citizenry also monetizes labour relations. Commitment and identity are bartered for monetary return, thus contaminating this last 'greenhouse'.

The Struggle for Involvement at the Expense of Others versus the Struggle for a Society with Room for Everyone: Future Scenarios

As more human beings are reduced to mere *homo oeconomicus* and economic and social exclusion becomes more extensive, deprivation is also on the rise. As a *homo oeconomicus* excluded from the 'total market' a person is objectively situated outside the market and thus is no longer a citizen, he is nobody. Subjectively and on the basis of society's supreme values he is seen as inefficient and reduced to nothing on this value scale. It can be argued that due to his own inefficiency he was unable to achieve the dominant ideology's maximum ideals. Young people and especially young women are the first to feel the impact of shrinking job opportunities. Lack of both esteem and self-esteem are an important product of their noninvolvement. Expectations from the past that include greater levels of involvement have prompted reflections on the nature of society and human beings, providing a good opportunity for critical examination of society but also entailing certain political risks.

It is encouraging to witness this discussion about our society and people's place within it. These reflections are essential to finding vindicatory answers to increasing exclusion that has resulted in a loss of place and identity. Such critical examination entails questioning the exclusionary system, and can bring us closer to building a society with room enough for everyone. However, an identity crisis does not imply *a priori* that the system is facing a legitimacy crisis. Critical reflections on the legitimacy of exclusion do not necessarily mean questioning that of the system as a whole. The danger of vindicating the legitimacy of involvement without questioning the system is that it can quickly lead to 'legitimizing' the exclusion of others, and thus the failure to address the root of the problem. Quite the contrary. Substituting an exclusionary model based on market mechanisms for another based on membership in a given community – cultural, racial, etc. – further dehumanizes social relations. Human beings do not unite in solidarity to demand a society where there is room enough for everyone, but they will fight over the increasingly fewer places. Fearful of losing their positions they will be even more adamant defending their own involvement, even at the expense of others.

Those newly excluded who until recently had benefited from and identified with the market-based system and its legitimating electoral process develop a deep sense of resentment at being left out. Failure to understand the root of the problem, in other words legitimizing the system, can lead to demands and justifications for using extra-economic means to gain access to possibilities for involvement that have been eliminated, even at the expense of others. Who are these newly excluded people? The social welfare state is giving way throughout the world to another that abstains as much as possible from any intervention in the market. This has led to the growing exclusion of public sector employees around the world. Obviously they are not the only sector comprising this new group. Unskilled workers in big industry had achieved relatively emancipated positions during the Keynesian period, at least in advanced countries. Now these workers are being excluded as industrial capital migrates to the periphery where labour reproduction costs are much lower. This often results in criticism of exclusion but does not necessarily extend to the system as such.

Those still employed represent a dwindling subpopulation, making them all the more replaceable. They become still more expensive if social contracts must continue to be respected instead of allowing the market to operate freely. They are considered pampered, inflexible and immovable due to anachronistic market rigidity mandating compliance with collective agreements and social welfare. Less state intervention leads to greater labour mobility and more flexibility in hiring, replacement and exclusion. Here the neoliberal motto 'more market and less government' reins supreme, resulting in fewer rights and thus less citizenry.

In Latin America exclusion is structural, as are economic and social insecurity. Low-skilled workers have always been highly replaceable and structurally excluded from employment and from economic and social security. Deep down the long-time excluded – such as women and 'minorities', among others – have never been a real part of the system, in other words they have never been true citizens. In contrast to the newly excluded, their demands for involvement are not usually developed at the expense of others. Never having been a real part of it before they now demand a society that has room for everyone, as was the case, for example, of the Zapatista movement in Chiapas, Mexico in 1994 (Espinoza, 1996). Indigenous peoples have never belonged in this system, they have never been citizens – they did not even have *cédulas*, the official identity cards – and they have had to develop survival strategies outside the system. For that reason they have been able to articulate a programme for the future: a society with room enough for everyone.

Totalization of the market and increasing structural exclusion go hand in hand. The erosion of protectionist measures in Latin America has led to reduction of industrial activities serving the domestic market that had employed much skilled labour. The so-called economic opening also stimulated the development of other industries – especially maquila – by transnational capital in search of cheaper less-skilled workers. Skilled labour has been replaced by unskilled labour throughout the hemisphere, increasing the replaceability of the middle class and not resolving unskilled workers' expendability. As a result, the middle class, and especially its young people, are now more replaceable and are losing rights and thus citizenship as well. This has led many to question the system of social welfare that had previously benefited them. The neoliberal perspective sees this sector as pampered, inflexible, and immovable according to the previously mentioned anachronistic rigidities (Chomsky and Dietrich, 1995: 107–10).

The Limits of Geopolitics without Citizens

This is not the first tide of newly excluded people in modern history, but this time it is occurring on a global scale. Fascism was built in the 1920s and 1930s on a foundation of exclusion. With the recent globalization of exclusion the re-emergence of fascism cannot be ruled out. In most countries that have experienced a resurgence of newly excluded people's movements – especially in the West – neofascist movements have also emerged to defend their places and identities even at the expense of others, fostering racism and xenophobia. Where structural possibilities for involvement are less developed there are fewer prospects for fascism and more for movements aiming to build a society with room enough for everyone.

The question then becomes: what type of social struggles will arise in our globalized world? Neofascist movements are very different when they are part of a broader bourgeois project. Exclusion affects not only popular sectors, but also entire countries and even sectors of the bourgeoisie. A bourgeoisie that has lost its global competitiveness will be excluded, and when feeling threatened like this it will fight to keep its place if at all possible, even at the expense of others. It easily becomes a struggle that transcends national borders.

Liberalism hit bottom during the crisis of the 1930s with the stock market crash and the ruin of many companies. Since it was no longer useful to the bourgeoisie it was substituted by nationalist protectionism. Corporate, authoritarian and antidemocratic state power was born, based on the same atomizing individualism that characterized economic liberalism. The bourgeoisie capitalized on populist demands for grassroots-level corporative involvement in a corporative state project. Nonexclusion of a nation's chosen people depended on its bourgeoisie's nonexclusion from international competition. During the worldwide depression fascist populist programmes were sidelined by the bourgeoisie's project to survive this shipwreck on an iceberg. As the bourgeoisie's economic policies floundered in one nation after another and even the largest companies began to sink, they resorted to extra-economic means and justified the extermination of entire peoples.

This was the case, for example, of Nazism and the Second World War. Greater awareness of the need for solidarity and possibilities of involvement as a means to resolve the crisis did not develop until after the war (Gombeaud and Décaillot, 1997: 206–7).

The spectre of economic depression looms over the world today, threatening even the largest transnational corporations, but this time the economic arenas' size has changed. The advent of FDI has helped to break down the formerly marked borders throughout the world and the so-called private borderless states without citizens have emerged. With the possible exception of the USA, it is unlikely that any nation can still provide the objective conditions needed for capital to reclaim its interests. Transnational capital has reached such levels of development that it now incorporates dominant interests that transcend borders – the best expression of this is the European Union. A more complex and also less visible web has been developed. FDI flows between Europe and the USA integrate transatlantic interests, as in the case of airline mergers involving companies from both sides. In other sectors such as aeroplane manufacture, however, there has been a clash of interests. Hegemony for some sectors lies on one side of the Atlantic and for others on the other. Private borderless states without citizens cannot become autarchic due to the relative levels of specialization, and there are no citizens linked to any of the sectors. In other words, there can be no geopolitical conflict among different transnationals' interests without political mediation.

The East–West and transatlantic situations are very different. Japanese FDI has penetrated both Western blocs much more extensively than is true for the reverse case. Eastern private borderless states have achieved greater influence on the West than Western ones on the East. The West has been very troubled by the loss of its competitive edge over the East and the resulting exclusion of one bourgeoisie by another in certain sectors. The considerable weight of productive sectors in the East has brought higher growth and allowed heavier investment that can improve their competitive edge through technology and acquisitions. The greatest protectionism – identification with the state and solidarity within an Asian society, meaning that their citizenry remained intact – gave them an important advantage over the West.

This leads us to closer examination of the Asian crisis, manifest since mid-1997 and the cause of great concern throughout the financial world. A financial cyclone has torn through the world since October 1997, troubling stock markets and heralding the increasingly real possibility of a major worldwide crash. On 27 October 1997 the New York stock exchange's primary index plummeted 554 points, the largest drop in points in its entire history, in a trading session that was cut short to avoid panic on Wall Street.

The Dow Jones Index fell 554 points or 7.2% reaching a new low since early May 1997, a full 16% lower than its peak in August. To understand the impact of this event bear in mind that on Black Monday in 1987, in what was the largest drop in Wall Street history, the Dow Jones fell 22.6%. In 1929 it had dropped 40% over a three-week period and over half of all stock brokerages failed in the following weeks (Aglietta, 1979: 319–21). A recurrence of this scenario remains a possibility and would mean destruction of the neoliberal house, leaving no clear prospects as to future scenarios.

These financial worries would seem to stem from the Southeast Asian monetary crisis. The crash of the all-important Hong Kong stock exchange on Thursday 23 October was triggered by government efforts to contain speculation against the Hong Kong dollar that had been fixed to the US dollar. The fiasco began when the government spent part of its international reserves and raised interest rates in a move to protect its currency. Large speculators such as George Soros, along with institutional investors, are able to obtain loans for billions of US dollars in local currency to purchase other currencies using that virtual money, thus provoking a devaluation.

The government of the country in crisis attempts to purchase its currency using its international US dollar reserves. After these are depleted the local currency is devalued and speculators again purchase it at this much lower rate, thus acquiring that country's foreign reserves. It then has no alternative but to resort to the IMF, comply with IMF adjustment policies and open its borders to transnational and especially US capital. The impact on stock markets is soon felt, as are the loss of confidence, capital flight and the immediate sell-off of stocks. The Hong Kong stock market plummeted 10.4% in just one day and 23% in less than a week.

The Asian monetary crisis had begun earlier with an apparently isolated attack against the Thai currency, which had been targeted by financial speculators. Its declining balance of payments had alerted the country to the devaluation. Since July Thailand had depleted its international reserves and quit defending its currency, which in four months had dropped from 25 to 40 bahts per US dollar. Malaysia was the next victim of this assault on Asian currencies. South Korea's central bank gave up defending its currency, the won, on 17 November 1997 and it quickly fell in less than a month from 900 in mid-October to 1,130 per US dollar (Sapford and Williams, 1997: B5).

The USA did not provide these Asian countries with aid as they had to Mexico when its crisis broke out in 1994–95. This crisis actually worked to their advantage by helping them 'cage the tigers' with IMF-imposed structural adjustment policies and control mechanisms to effectively open these protected markets (Sender, 1997: 69). The destabilization in some of these countries triggered the spontaneous flight of foreign reserves throughout the region. One after another these Asian bloc countries were forced to seek IMF help, whose conditions included opening their markets to foreign investment. As Asia's major financier, Japan has felt the impact more recently. The Nikkei Index dropped 20% between 1 August and 1 November while the Nikkei Banking Index fell 30%. Two of Japan's ten largest banks were even forced into bankruptcy (Sapford and Williams, 1997: 5B).

The Asian financial crisis must be understood in the context of the economic world war over markets unable to accommodate all transnational corporations. As pointed out by Engelhard (1997), the third world war has begun. As the market has become more global and as it has penetrated more and more aspects of life, the primary weapons being used are increasingly economic ones. Territorial occupation is no longer needed to control nations. With this attack on Southeast Asia's financial system, the West and the USA in particular showed that in this world without room enough for all TNCs the Western ones will take their place even at the expense of Eastern ones. However, these financial weapons are also potentially self-destructive. Destabilizing Asian currencies risks extending the financial crisis to the rest of the world as well. The stock market crash impacted on Latin America as an emergent market, but the psychological impact was truly felt after it hit the emergent Russian market.

Latin America suffered the effects of these financial and stock market tensions. In the week of 24–30 October 1997 the Brazilian and

Argentine stock exchanges closed with losses of 23.3% and 19.6% respectively (Greg, 1997: 25A). Brazil faced an especially difficult situation. Its substantial fiscal and trade deficits and overvalued exchange rate made it seem a likely target for speculators' next assault. However, Russia jumped ahead in the chain of financial destabilization, reactivating Latin America's financial crisis and sparking fears of a worldwide depression similar to that of the 1930s.

With the destabilization of Latin American currencies, Brazil drastically raised interest rates and resorted to using its international reserves. The Brazilian stock market promptly began to fall, further deepening financial instability throughout Latin America and the world and adding to international investors' financial panic. These crises are becoming less and less isolated and although the direct effects of destabilization seem to have already occurred, its indirect effects only began to appear in the second half of 1998. Initially bets were being placed on probable winners from the West and mostly in Western currencies rather than Japanese yen, resulting in a Westernization of the global casino. At first glance, the prospects for the West seemed very promising. However, the global economy as a whole has slowed considerably. The locomotive driving the world economy was lost in Asia's economic slowdown. Southeast Asia's internal demand is expected to plummet over the next few years, resulting in a marked (over)supply of goods in the world market and sparking a general deflation (Chesnais, 1998: 18). This would lead to a decline in real profits and would dash all hope that gambles on prospects of future gains might actually pay off. This crisis would cause a worldwide financial panic that was already foreshadowed in October 1998. The crisis of neoliberalism had begun.

Worldwide Recession and the Necessary Shift away from Neoliberalism

News of neoliberalism's plunge into crisis was widely proclaimed as large transnational corporations' profits began to plummet – a true sign of this crisis that was declared in October 1998. Indeed, only when transnational profits are endangered does this model truly enter into crisis. During the absolute reign of the invisible hand over the economy, transnational capital focused its investments on securing world markets. These economic disputes resulted in the so-called private borderless states that have come to predominate over nation-states. The trend is for a few of these private borderless states to use planning more and more within their own borders reducing the market to an ever smaller proportion of the global product. Planning is gradually replacing the market.

Although planning is becoming much more important, the war for maximization of profits continues in the name of market economy efficiency. Investment in acquisitions, mergers and privatization develops competitive market positions but does not create wealth. Higher transnational profits and expectations aroused by mergers fuel the stock market. The distance between real values and stock prices continues to increase. The financial market is transformed into a real global casino with few players. Twenty-five years ago 90% of capital involved in international trade were productive and commercial investments while only 10% were speculative. An UNCTAD report estimates that by the mid-1990s 95% were involved in speculation. Nobel Prize-winning economist James Tobin warned that these speculative investment flows would result in negative worldwide economic growth. He urged the use of taxation to curb this trend since otherwise the spiral of inequality would continue unchecked – in the USA by 1995 it had matched 1929 levels. Sooner or later this would result in a stock market crash and the collapse of big capital's profits (Chomsky and Dietrich, 1995: 41.89).

Disparity among fortunes has reached unprecedented levels leading to the insolvency of ever-broader sectors that now include entire nations as well as increasingly strong capital groups. If banks would stop lending to non-credit-worthy sectors they could effectively protect their financial structures but would be left with increasingly fewer suitable places to make loans. Banks do have the obligation to pay interest to depositors and so must also extend loans, but in a climate of widespread declining solvency more and more of these loans are questionable. This increases the possibility of bank failures and the deterioration of the financial system as a whole. As investment becomes riskier higher benefits are expected in return, thus decreasing aversion to these speculative gambles. If monetary policies manage to control low interest rates more investments will be made in the stock market, which in turn will become more speculative. Some will win and others will lose and while no social wealth is created it is rapidly concentrated. The obsession with ever-higher profits tends to draw investments farther away from productive spheres. As the speculative bubble grows market values lose all relation to their real values and at any moment it can burst. A crash in the world market would bring the ruin of many large corporations and distrust of the financial system, resulting in a significant economic contraction and decline in employment that would last for years – a global depression.

Before October 1998 economists did not believe another depression was possible, and they still claim that scientific knowledge and adequate management can effectively avoid such an event. They are, however, failing to consider the roots of this eventual depression – an impossibility for them since it would also require they examine the roots of the concentration of wealth, and question the very legitimacy of neoliberal ideology and the system as a whole. The issue is not whether there will be a depression. Even assuming that it could be avoided by a 'soft landing', the downward spiral of economic growth would remain unresolved. Recessions are becoming longer and deeper in more and more places while economic recovery has become slower and shorter and occurs in fewer and fewer places.

Although it is not yet a global depression, this situation is affecting more and broader strata that have long been pillars of the current market system (Wallerstein, 1989: 10–17). A growing segment of transnationals has even been affected in this latest phase, as is the current case in Asia. There is also an underlying threat of general crisis within the private borderless states. All this leads to the possibility of a general worldwide legitimacy crisis.

Faced with this imminent crisis, now is the time to make a strong stand and demand the obligatory shift away from neoliberalism and a return to the visible hand. This time it could and should be given a global rather than national reach. Intervention on a nation-state level is no longer sufficient. It must operate on a global scale to regulate the invisible hand that is directing private borderless states without citizens towards the exclusionary casino economy and forfeiture of well-being. The time has come to establish a global social contract and work to build a world with room enough for everyone. It is no longer sufficient for a visible hand to guide the invisible one. The historical moment has come for the visible hand to take control and reorganize market relations to reintegrate them with people's lives.

Towards Worldwide Regulation Based on the Global Common Good

How should the line be drawn between subordinating efficiency to vitality or vitality to efficiency? The predominant school of economic thought in the period immediately following the 1930s crisis represents a synthesis of a macroanalytical defence of the Common Good and traditional micro-level thought endorsing the purportedly nonweighted sum of private interests. This synthesis provided the foundation for Keynesianism, although it is important to remember that it was firmly based on the theory of rational decision-making and thus, in the last instance, was always centred on private interests rather than the citizenry. Keynesians hold that supply and demand are determined by rational decisions and at the same time attempt to explain and resolve employment, inflation and economic cycles on a macro level.

Neoclassical and monetarist approaches are entirely grounded in rational decision-making theory, which leads them to explain these same three phenomena as the result of disturbances in optimum resource allocation caused by chance or external intervention. Monetarists locate the causes of unemployment and inflation outside the market and business world. Keynesians accept the existence of imperfections within the market system and argue that state intervention and regulation are needed. Monetarists, on the other hand, claim that government intervention impedes optimum market performance and that all obstacles should be removed and state intervention dismantled. They argue that by no means should new or intensified forms of intervention be established. Neoliberals claim that this is precisely what is needed to build the best of all possible worlds (Nell, 1996: 22–5).

Classical economists, such as Smith, Ricardo, and Marx, along with their contemporary representatives, see the market as a combat arena instead of a mechanism for optimum resource allocation. It was a stage for the struggle over distribution of wealth and according to Nell (ibid.) competition was a sort of war over resource allocation. The losers faced bankruptcy and the winners received even more wealth. Competition was a constantly changing scenario in the long run. The number of businesses fell over time and some expanded at the expense of others. Monopolies were formed and ideal competition became a thing of the past. The market's so-called imperfections had become structural over time, giving a decided competitive edge to the bigger players. The primary economic agents no longer operate in the world under given circumstances as explained in textbooks. They now intervene in the political economy of nation-states, even subordinating them to their own interests. As the strongest players they benefit greatly from *laissez faire*. Circumstances may have been a determining factor for all businesses in the ideal competition-based economy of 150 years ago, but that is no longer the case. Nell (ibid.: 37–8) concludes that economists who still endorse these dated assumptions are completely incapable of understanding the real economy of today's world.

An economic theory restricted to analysing optimum resource allocation under given circumstances without considering that which indicates the best ways to change those circumstances has lost historical perspective. The notion that in a market economy maximization of all private companies' interests will lead to the Common Good directed by an invisible hand is sheer dominant ideology benefiting TNCs.

Keynes (1936: 378) stated that his criticism was aimed not at the internal logic of established economic theory, but rather at those assumptions that were rarely satisfied at that time. He thought that by establishing a determined aggregate demand – through state intervention – resource allocation would be optimally regulated by the market. This reasoning points to the problem but fails to cover it completely. It is not sufficient to guarantee the scale of demand. Its composition must also be defined. Greater state support of the demand for production equipment – including the military – coupled with retention of the demand for consumer goods leads to high unused capacity and contraction of future demand. In that sense, Nell (1996: 61) claims it is impossible to accept the invisible hand notions of either Adam Smith or of Keynes.

Widespread high idle capacity results in more aggressive competition for this restricted demand. The invisible hand thus shifts towards lower levels of growth and employment. Individual companies invest in technology in order to use resources as efficiently as possible. System-wide this results in more unused capacity, in other words in inefficient allocation of resources on the level of society as a whole, according to Nell (ibid.). A state-defined aggregate demand that stimulates demand for production goods more than for consumer ones is merely reinforcing capital's natural tendency – to foment more idle capacity and thus a drop in demand, demonstrating the inefficiency of state intervention. Instead of redefining state intervention, economic doctrine moved towards neoliberalism and its much-heralded free market efficiency. Contrary to Rousseau's claims (1950: 196/93) the Common Good or collective volition is not to be found in the summed and weighted individual good or the weighted volition of private initiatives. On the other hand, an economy that subordinates efficiency to vitality can use resources fully and without waste on the level of the system as a whole (Nell, 1996: 97). To state that if a system as a whole functions with vitality then each of its parts will be efficient is as untrue as its inverse – that if each of the parts is efficient then the system as a whole will have vitality.

An individual company must operate more efficiently to improve its own standing, but to improve the economic system as a whole it must operate with vitality rather than efficiency. Vitality is associated with reproduction of the real economy and building a future world for real human beings with concrete needs, whereas efficiency leads to destruction of the whole. As long as the system as a whole is thought to operate largely the same as its parts it will be nearly impossible to find a solution to the problem of restricted demand and the system will lose vitality. To regain vitality the system must be considered as a whole and individual interests subordinated to the Common Good, and it must not allow the imposition of summed and poorly weighted individual interests. In order to understand these policies defined in terms of the whole we must first consider what now makes up this whole at the turn of the millennium. Neither it nor the Common Good can still be defined as they were 50 years ago.

As national economies are increasingly and significantly integrated through trade and FDI into the world market, the nation can no longer be considered as the whole. Increasingly the world market has come to constitute the whole and each nation has become a part of that system, even though each of these parts is also a whole. If, for example, each nation were to reach a balance between exports and imports, then demand would adjust to meet the needs of nations less favoured in terms of exports. A decrease in imports by weaker nations would lead to a corresponding decline in exports from stronger ones, causing a drop in worldwide demand and slowdown of domestic activity. Free trade leads to efficiency of the strongest individual companies but not to the global Common Good (Nell, 1996: 103). The Common Good must be defined in terms of the world economy as a whole.

Globalization and World Citizenry: A Regulatory Void

From the perspective of the world economy it would be rational to increase demand, but since government leaders are subjected to the individual interests of private borderless states they advocate austerity instead. It would seem logical to reduce spending in times of crisis and that would be the case for individuals taken alone or as a group, but not for the economy as a whole. A nation cannot prosper by impoverishing its people. A generalized government austerity programme is thus the wrong economic policy for a world economy in crisis even though, while it lasted, it could lead to prosperity – concentration and centralization of capital – for private borderless states. Nation-states' current economic policies are no longer based on promoting the country's growth or well-being; they are now more concerned with avoiding the negative effects of the crisis on their economies (Holloway et al., 1995: 113).

A policy for system-wide austerity would not improve the balance of payments for any country, even though individually such policies could achieve this for a given country. It would result in a general contraction and downward spiral of international trade. Neoliberal economists' prescriptions for austerity lead to contraction of demand and of economic growth. Government austerity curbs real demand but strengthens the free market in the hands of private borderless states. This leads to centralization and concentration of capital in fewer transnational hands at the expense of the vitality of the system as a whole.

As expectations of future demand decrease, so too will productive investments as well as total profit mass and profit rates. Profit expectations in the productive sphere continue to decline. Financial and speculative investment becomes the primary arena for high-yield profits. Financial investing is a sterile activity that produces neither goods nor value and operates at the expense of the system's vitality. Economists and government leaders, however, think that what is good for them as individuals is also good for the system. Capital is concerned with maximization of profit but not its origin. Profit without growth is only possible through concentration of wealth or speculation. Maximization of gains by increasing concentration ultimately leads to one recession after another. Governments are subordinate to transnational financial capital and as long as the Common Good continues to be perceived as the sum of private interests they will be unable to find a way out of the crisis and will be limited to avoiding its negative affects.

In the first years following the Second World War, governments could still rely on short-term financial capital movements for the primary purpose of ensuring the maximum viability of economic autonomy and avoiding the sacrifice of economic interdependence. They still had the tools to provide economic vitality. However, between the mid-1970s and mid-1990s a broad movement of capital has extracted itself from state control and formed a series of networks through which TNCs and the big banks move capital throughout the entire world. Each private borderless state has organized a sort of internal financial market, preferably located in some fiscal haven from which to channel their direct investments and remittances with no concern for national interests. The rapid growth of financial innovations simultaneously produced an enormous paper economy in search of profit rates no longer available in the real economy, moving unprecedented amounts of capital every day unconstrained by time of day or distances (Goodmann and Pauly, 1993: 72).

Financial markets tore down national financial barriers while moving substantial resources for TNCs involved with globalization, increasing their ability to develop foreign investment and remittance evasion strategies. First, governments realized that to be effective controls must continually be reinforced, but they later discovered that the results or potential economic costs of maintaining them far outweighed their benefits. National interest was subordinated to that of private states, and first of all to the field of financial capital (Ianni, 1996: 9.40).

Strictly speaking the internationalization of capital also entails the formation of global capital, a new and developed form of general capital. It develops alongside individual and private capital – national and sectorial – subordinating and redefining them. Individual and private forms of capital located in national and sectorial contexts are subordinate to general capital forms found in the transnational arena. Although there are frequent reciprocal congruities, concurrence, and convergence among national governments and businesses, corporations or conglomerates with respect to national, regional and global issues TNCs have irrefutably broken free from the impositions and limitations intrinsic to national states.

The geo-economy and geopolitics of private borderless states and of national states do not always coincide and frequently are separate or even conflicting. The conditions and possibilities for sovereignty, a national agenda, national emancipation, and institutional reform are now determined by the needs of multilateral or global institutions, organizations, and corporations existing over and beyond nations. The state apparatus is reorganized following the new requirements of markets, factors of production flows and strategic alliances among corporations that all operate on a global scale. This leads to the internationalization of guidelines regarding deregulation, privatization, opening borders and the like (Ianni, 1996: 33).

National political economy has become less autonomous. Even national currency is now controlled and manipulated by market forces. Financial capital has become stronger as it has become more independent from the nation-state. The rise of financial capital has caused a shift in the centre of political and economic power away from the nation-state, though it is not to be found at TNCs' executive headquarters either. Financial markets regulate the real power and the occupants of those executive headquarters spend days compiling financial statements in order to improve their stocks' market prices. Ownership and control of TNCs is now in the form of financial assets managed by financial corporations such as pension funds, which ultimately are ruled by the financial market's ups and downs (Ianni, 1996: 41). Supply and demand are the primary force in this financial market and are where the global management crisis is most apparent (Andreff, 1995: 112).

New global regulations must be enacted here more than in any other field in order to control the risks inherent to a global financial market (Ianni, 1996: 127). This would require a new philosophy giving precedence to the whole over the interests of private borderless states, and for that to occur the crisis would have to dramatically affect transnational capital. In this sense environmental deterioration and destruction or the increasing exclusion and impoverishment of the world's people are of little consequence. The crisis becomes real for big capital only when its businesses and properties begin to crumble – in other words, global depression. That is when the world economy makes its presence felt.

The depressed world economy can only appear to establish a general sense of identification with the Common Good of the entire planet – world citizenry – in other words, when private borderless states are also in crisis. When the sum of private interests leads to the Common Bad for everyone, including TNCs, the need for a world organization capable of subordinating the interests of private borderless states to the planetary Common Good will become dramatically apparent (Roustang et al., 1996: 70). Ironically, neoliberalism has destroyed most economic regulatory mechanisms. In a global depression this void will appear as the terrible force behind the economically, politically and socially insecure scene. These circumstances would be ripe for alternative forms of involvement for some cultures or nations at the expense of everyone else thus endangering attempts to build a globally regulated and inclusive globalization with room enough for all.

6

Towards a Citizen-based Alternative

In this chapter I propose a citizen-based alternative to neoliberalism. This is a logical consequence of the analysis developed in the preceding chapters and represents a possible and plausible historical scenario. This is not a concrete alternative involving explicit policy proposals for some future government agenda. A theoretical framework provides the foundation on which to formulate concrete but not arbitrary initiatives. It is grounded in a citizen-led, totality-based response to neoliberalism. The central proposal focuses on devising a way to reconcile private interests and the Common Good without the latter becoming subordinated, in the last instance, to the market.

Growing Awareness of Neoliberalism's Limitations

Although alternatives to neoliberalism are still almost nonexistent in mainstream thought, there has been growing uncertainty since late 1997 regarding the world economy's shift towards increasing deregulation, which intensified with the onset of the Russian financial crisis in late August 1998. This concern coincides with two important events. The Asian crisis that began in mid-1997 seemingly became global when the Russian financial crisis broke out a year later. On a less apparent level, the proposed Multilateral Agreement on Investment (MAI) suffered a serious setback in April 1998 as a result of the growing citizens' movements. These sparked renewed debate on possible new models of economic regulation on a global scale (Meiksins Wood, 1997: 1–17; Fouquet and Lemaître, 1997; Coutrot, 1998: 253–64; Kolo, 1998: 7; Ramonet, 1998: 9; Cassen, 1998: 10).

Until recently globalization and elimination of the state's role were generally thought to be inevitable, even among those on the left. After October 1997, the Asian crisis and opposition to the MAI project represent a shift in the state's role in deregulation. After MAI had been postponed for a year, transnational corporations suffered a serious setback at the hands of OECD member nation-states seeking to defend themselves from an imminent loss of self-determination. This shift eventually marked the beginning of a new era of regulation.

Concern about consequences beyond the region has sparked growing criticism of the IMF and its handling of the Asian crisis since late 1997. Multi-millionaire financier George Soros and the finance ministers from the Group of Seven countries (G-7) as well as scholars such as Harvard professor Jeffrey Sachs, have all been harshly critical of the IMF (Kolo, 1998: 7). Even *Foreign Affairs*, a journal representing the US intellectual elite, has joined in this chorus. Feldstein (1998: 32) argues that the IMF has not acted to prevent the monetary crisis in the Asian bloc but has actually fuelled financial instability in the region in order to open their capital markets to foreign – Western – capital. As the effects of the crisis have spread beyond Asia itself, the IMF's definition of its role and its approach to affected countries' problems have endangered its own effectiveness (Feldstein, 1998: 22).

Coutrot (1998: 259) points out that until now international monetary authorities have been able to prevent local monetary and stock market crises from spreading throughout the world, but it is doubtful they will be as successful in the future. In fact, the real possibility of a worldwide financial crisis was first revealed by the crash in Asia and the chain reaction provoked throughout the region and beyond by the Russian crisis and the very real threat in Latin America. The Asian crash is the first crisis of globalization (Gréau, 1998: 374). It is a classic crisis of private sector overinvestment and overindebtedness that is typical of long economic cycles but not of uncontrolled public debt, as was the case in Latin America. Thus it would be pointless for the IMF to continue to impose measures used in Latin America on Asia (Gréau, 1998: 375).

Until 1997 the continued expansion of production in Asia represented 50% of the world's economic growth and two-thirds of world trade (Rohwer, 1998: 22), resulting in the overestimation of this market's potential size and a flood of easy credit from international banks into the region (Gréau, 1998: 376). In the 1990s, Japan's economic slump and increasing competition from China limited their possibilities for commercial realization. Attacks on local currencies soon followed, since under such circumstances it was impossible to maintain their parity with the US dollar. As the breakdown spread throughout the region, the IMF did not intervene to offset the most serious effects as it had in Mexico. Quite the contrary. This far-reaching chain reaction triggered fears that the crisis could spread to the rest of the world, as had occurred with the Russian crisis, and actually set off a global depression.

Authors such as Gréau (1998) and Fox (1998) have argued that the US economy is a sort of Achilles' heel for world crisis. US economic growth is largely based on using private household debt to maintain strong domestic demand. This private debt is largely derived from stock acquisitions (Fox, 1998: 52) and prior to the market's collapse had generated income. This debt and the income derived from it reached their limit with the stock market crash and the decline in domestic demand. External demand also fell as US exports dropped 8% in the second quarter of 1998. Although exports represented only 13% of the US GDP they were an important factor in general economic growth and transnational profits in particular (Fox, 1998: 52).

On the other hand, deflation has caused imports to become more competitive. This process, triggered by Asia's financial crisis, has rocked Japan, Russia and Latin America, and is threatening the USA and Europe as well. Rohwer has pointed out (1998: 22) that it could become the most widespread and severe deflation since the Great Depression of the 1930s, even resulting in a global recession.

A slump in US economic growth would probably trigger an abrupt drop in its highly overvalued stock market prices, as well as economic destabilization and uncertainty around the world (Gréau, 1998: 382). What could be the impact of such a crash? In 1995, before the Asian crisis, profits of the Fortune 500 companies increased 13.5% and the Dow Jones Index rose 33%. In 1997 these business profits fell 7.8% but the stock market continued to rise another 23%. In other words, the gap between real and nominal profits widened. The largest corporations are clearly facing a slump in their real profits (Nocera, 1998: 42). Nocera argues that the Dow Jones Index will drop to less than 5,300, allowing it to adjust to its historical average growth. The psychology of speculating on the decline could lead it to fall to as low as 4,000, less than half of its early 1998 levels (Nocera, 1998: 44). Deflation, which is becoming more severe as more countries fall into crisis, is affecting the proceeds of 1998 business profits. A drop in real profits could lead to a real stock market crash around the world and global recession (Fox, 1998: 52).

Under such uncertain circumstances, it is not surprising that conservative thought has been increasingly critical of neoliberalism's disastrous effects. In *Foreign Affairs*, Feldstein (1998: 20–3) directly criticizes the dangers posed by the IMF's role in deregulation and the ensuing destabilization resulting from the Asian crisis. Similarly, renowned London School of Economics professor John Gray (1998) has argued that unrestricted free market forces lead to disaster. For many years it was believed that markets would work their magic and resolve economic problems. It also seemed that the world was immersed in an endless free market period. But now with the threat of global collapse that is no longer the case (Fox, 1998: 54). Until recently the world did not seem to need strong leaders. Now they are sorely needed to help get the world back on track, but are in very short supply.

Similarly, World Trade Organization architect Peter Sutherland along with W. Sewell (Sewell and Sutherland, 1998) argues that greater worldwide cooperation is needed to prevent the otherwise impending crash that will result from unregulated competition. On a different level, the secretary of the OECD has called attention to the social tensions triggered by globalization, and particularly to the rapidly rising wage inequalities potentially threatening social stability (ILO, 1997: 8).

Even the IMF has implicitly questioned neoliberal policies as reflected, for example, in a February 1998 report analysing the impact of structural adjustment policies on low-income countries. It concludes that, even controlling for demographic effects, economic performance – per capita growth and foreign debt as related to GDP, among others – in countries not subjected to these policies has been better than in those where they have been applied (Kolo, 1998: 7).

The MAI was presented to OECD member states for approval in late 1997, amid increasing criticism of neoliberalism. The response to this declaration of the universal rights of capital demonstrated member states' unwillingness to abandon their defence of the Common

Good to transnational companies' unlimited ambitions (Cassen, 1998: 11). The initiative was meant to limit the self-determination of nation-states – including industrialized countries – in strategic matters, and to favour transnationals by creating a series of international rules granting TNCs *de jure* powers that would place them above nation-states. Its approval would have formally eradicated nation-states' self-determination regarding strategic economic issues.

Significantly, the MAI initiative was not passed in April 1998 and was postponed for at least one year. Low-income country governments first expressed concern regarding its negative impact in Singapore in November 1996 (Wesselius, 1998: 8). Following the Asian crisis in late 1997, a growing number of NGOs from the North have expressed anger over its possibly devastating impact on their own societies, the environment and consumer interests. Increasing criticism within civil society has led more legislators to demand that their governments study the MAI more closely. Finally, the ministers met in Paris and decided to postpone its approval for one year (*Revista del Sur*, April 1998: 9).

The MAI's failure to win approval was a political setback for neo-liberals. In the past, the nation-state had acted under strong pressure from transnationals to deregulate the world economy. Now, these same nation-states are under strong pressure from the world's citizenry to halt that deregulation at all costs. The lack of support for the MAI revealed that economic rationality is neither mechanical nor inevitable. It showed that society could influence certain economic behaviours. Neoliberals will surely look to new forums, such as the WTO or the IMF, for support of this initiative. But citizen pressure will not end here, argues Cassen (1998: 11), while there is still a chance to reclaim – at least as a new Utopia – an MAI that is grounded in citizen rights and investors' obligations to beneficiary countries.

Postponing this initiative's implementation demonstrated that the deregulation inherent in globalization depends on joint intervention by states to defend TNC interests as they attempt to formalize free market regulations in a climate increasingly critical of neoliberalism. The opposition is working to avert this international state consensus to approve the MAI by developing forces in every country. The worldwide network articulating this national opposition has received added support as the irrationality of and cracks in globalization become more apparent. If nation-states choose to follow neoliberalism's destructive logic despite its increasingly visible irrationality, domestic grassroots struggles against this unifying logic will represent the strongest platform from which to develop new internationalist alternatives (Meiksins Wood, 1997: 4, 6, 14).

Meiksins Wood has argued that the increasing competitiveness and neoliberal policies resulting from the political struggle surrounding the threat of world crisis are no longer seen as automatic, logical or inevitable results of globalization. Under such circumstances, the deliberate political struggle in support of transnational interests can be seen for what it really is – a struggle against the citizenry. The real problem with neoliberalism lies in the political control of the process rather than in the economy itself. National and global debate on this problem will become increasingly important in the near future.

In Search of the Common Good for Humanity

An alternative historical perspective to the predominant neoliberal approach views globalization from a critical stance. It is somewhat ironic, as Mortimer (1997: 14) has pointed out, that world capitalism's critical effects as described by Marx and Engels more than 150 years ago in the *Communist Manifesto* are proving true, at least in part, at a time when there are few remaining advocates of Marxism. The increasingly evident cracks in neoliberalism have shed light on new horizons, facilitating the difficult task of formulating alternatives.

Researchers with a commitment to the citizenry are questioning the end of history and focusing their efforts on developing historically grounded alternatives to neoliberalism. Authors such as Zevin (1992), Tabb (1997) and Rodrik (1997) have argued that globalization is neither new nor eternal. Their research has shown that the world economy was more open in 1875 than in 1975. International capital movements actually decreased during those one hundred years. Between these internationalized economy periods, the two world wars and the Great Depression of the 1930s gave rise to an intermediate period of national economies (Tabb, 1997: 24). This leads to the question of whether the world is perhaps on the threshold of a new period of regulation and, therefore, of hope.

The new model of economic regulation has been the focus of

ongoing debate since 1997 (Meiksins Wood 1997; Fouquet and Lemaître, 1997; Ngoc Liem, 1998; Gréau, 1998; Coutrot, 1998). Although debate over Keynesianism continues, the current effectiveness of these older forms of economic intervention has come under increasing scrutiny (Meiksins Wood, 1997: 15). After the Great Depression of the 1930s, Keynesian economic regulation played a key role in protecting capitalism from the system's self-destructive logic. 'Keynes' objective was to preserve the capitalist order' (Ngoc Liem, 1998: 151). He did not consider the possibility of a crisis caused by the inadequate allocation of profits in productivity among the players in business – in other words, among employers and workers. 'These were merely partial analyses of the capitalist economy's dysfunctions' (ibid.: 153).

The threat of another world depression has reinvigorated the debate regarding new economic regulation, this time on a global scale. During periods of economic openness, Keynesian policies attuned to the national economy are considered archaic. However, even then he called attention to the possibility of supranational coordination of economic policies that has now become more feasible. Keynes proposed using a supranational central bank and a single currency to coordinate world economic policies (ibid.: 150). In the 1930s, he also advocated shifting from a casino economy to one based on productive investment to avoid capital flight to the speculative sphere. These ideas are again being discussed as possible alternatives (Fouquet and Lemaître, 1997: 150).

We are at a historical juncture where the cracks in neoliberalism are beginning to show and the still somewhat timid worldwide citizens' organizations are beginning to question that model and suggest citizen-based alternatives. Given impending economic regulations, the question becomes whether political action can still take the form of economic intervention based on a conciliation of citizens' and private interests while respecting efficiency as the last word, in true Keynesian style. Or will this be a new type of economic regulation in which, as Meiksins Wood (1997: 15) proposes, political power will control capital movements and capital allocation and distribution of economic surplus will be regulated within a democratic framework of citizen-based social accountability?

Vitality over efficiency: towards a new economic regulation When efficiency, as the fundamental criterion of neoliberal economic performance, allows only chaotic, uneven and unequal growth, the discussion of alternatives becomes both politically and academically significant. To question this all-powerful efficiency means discussing alternatives to that economic rationality. Coutrot argues that:

> the criteria for economic efficacy are socially determined ... It depends on which criteria for efficacy are defined as priorities by a society at a given moment in history ... In fact there is no abstract definition of economic efficacy and ... predominance of one criterion – efficiency – over others – such as sustainability or consumer satisfaction – are not at all natural. They represent a social decision ... It is essential ... to regain political control of ongoing evolution. (Coutrot, 1998: 261–4)

Coutrot's concept of efficacy refers to the benefits of economic performance viewed by-content and through efficiency. It refers to the social form. He focuses on the academic and political debate on the benefits of a new economic rationality. By proposing economic re-regulation, Coutrot is suggesting the subordination – not suppression – of efficiency to other criteria of economic performance.

In a previous study (Dierckxsens, 1998: 29–55), economic rationality is examined using the double axis of efficiency and vitality. The scale from more to less economic regulation is located between the two axes (see Figure 6.1). The absolute primacy of efficiency leads to market totalization and imposition of individual interests at the expense of the citizenry's interests. The market is the single and ultimate regulatory mechanism. State and government intervention consists of promoting economic deregulation and absolute nonintervention.

Suppressing efficiency would seem to be a logical response to destructive liberalism. Developing vitality in this way, however, precludes any market mediation, leaving little or no margin for conciliation between private interests and the common good, as was the case of real socialism. Ties to private interests tend to disappear when the market economy is suppressed and the central plan becomes the single ultimate form of economic regulation. Everything is determined by the central plan and nothing is left to private initiative. The state becomes a huge bureaucratic apparatus in charge of its implementation. Rejecting the very basis of the market leads to its total suppression and to the unintended consequence of totalizing the plan

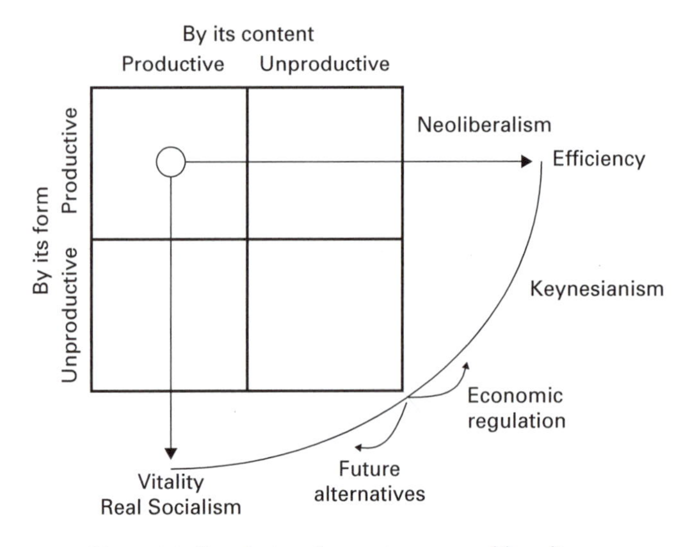

Figure 6.1 Regulative alternatives to neoliberalism

without any real democratic mediation. Another unintended effect is the substitution of the market's single voice for that of a single party that implements the plan in the name of the citizenry without any real communication between them.

Historically, Keynesianism represents the third slope between the two axes as it seeks to reconcile efficiency and vitality. It involves state conciliation of the citizenry's and private interests in the context of an essentially national economy. The legitimacy of Keynesian state intervention is based on its role as regulator of efficiency and vitality, but only so far as to protect the logic of capital accumulation. In other words, private interests outweigh the common good. The moment the nation-state no longer accomplishes this to the benefit of profit rates and capital accumulation it is delegitimized in the eyes of capital, as occurred in the 1970s.

Neoliberalism aimed to reclaim efficiency at the expense of the entire citizenry. Under this model efficiency became the determining factor. Efficiency and private interests were to be protected even at the expense of vitality and the common good. The neoliberal state was responsible for promoting economic deregulation and protecting efficiency. This even led to its 'voluntary and democratic' retreat in favour of transnationals, as suggested in the MAI. Giving absolute priority to efficiency at the expense of all other economic criteria results in an exclusionary and destabilizing form of capitalism. Sooner or later this will lead to a world crisis requiring a new model of economic regulation.

The crisis of neoliberalism reveals the need for a new model of economic intervention capable of regulating the space between private interests and the common good. It is neither probable nor possible to achieve vitality by totally eradicating efficiency. This would be just another totalizing response with historically well-known effects. Globalization that tries to achieve vitality at the expense of all private interests would turn out to be simply another alternative without citizenry. A logical historical outcome could involve the regulation of private interest and the common good where, in the last instance, vitality predominates over efficiency and the citizenry over private interests, without suppression of the latter. A sort of reverse Keynesianism could emerge in the near future, in which the social welfare state would be substituted by a solidarity state committed to serving the citizenry. This state would use regulation to benefit the Common Good. Private interests would be allowed to operate but not at the expense of the common good or the citizenry. The vitality of the whole would replace efficiency as the ultimate criterion.

Global regulation as an alternative to neoliberalism The existing economic rationality must be changed if the interests of the whole are to prevail over private interests. It is not enough to change capital's rationality in just one company, country or even one bloc. It would be suicidal unilaterally to renounce maximization of profits in a context ruled by efficiency. To invert economic rationality in some places but not in others would lead to the defeat of progressive forces, highlighting free market superiority even as that logic led to the destruction of the whole. The search for an alternative with a different economic rationality can be approached on the level of the parts, but actually to change the prevailing rationality it must include regulation of the whole – in other words, a planetary world citizenry. Not only has globalization made this possible in the abstract, but increasing contradictions are making it necessary as well.

Giving priority to the vitality of the whole requires a citizen-based, totality-centred approach rather than focusing on efficiency as defined by the parts. To achieve vitality of the whole, the casino economy must first be replaced by a reproductive one, as was also proposed in the 1930s (Fouquet and Lemaître, 1997: 150). The central question becomes how to redirect economic activity towards the content of wealth. What regulation would be needed? Is it possible and sufficient to implement measures such as audits of transnational companies and fiscal impositions to prevent speculation?

The 'Tobin tax', named after Nobel Prize-winner James Tobin, who designed it as a means of preventing speculative capital flows (Tobin, 1978), is the topic of much discussion. He reformulated the proposal in 1978 and again in 1984 and 1991. He recommended using the tax system to curb capital flight to the speculative sphere. Other authors have pointed out the need to eliminate tax havens and advocated the return to solidarity-based forms of retirement – distributive system – rather than capitalization-based speculative pension funds (Cassen, 1998: 11).

Capital flight to the speculative sphere does not result from inappropriate fiscal measures and thus applying other fiscal measures will not resolve the root of the problem. Competitiveness depends on increasing technological depreciation to such an extent that productivity tends to grow less than innovation costs, resulting in falling profit rates and a shift to speculative economy. Technological innovation using credit or government subsidies promotes chronic underutilization of installations and actually accelerates depreciation as occurred, for example, during the Keynesian period.

Given the neoliberal crisis, regulation of technological depreciation would seem to be the only alternative. This would involve intervention in the logic of capital, in its own rationality. Future regulation should and could intervene in the very heart of capital's logic, controlling the rate of depreciation (Meiksins Wood, 1997: 15). Just as international auditing firms such as Price Waterhouse or Pete Marwick perform ecological audits of transnational firms, such as Shell, they would be even better qualified to conduct audits regarding quantifiable matters such as technological depreciation. Such initiatives would be successful only if they were widespread, so future economic regulation must be global. In practice, it is sufficient to regulate depreciation and the resulting wastefulness in OECD countries where most TNCs are located. The richest 20% of the world consumes 80% of natural resources and 70% of energy (Martin and Schumann, 1996: 48).

Economic regulation: the driving force behind a new economic rationality The use of audits and/or fiscal measures on a global scale to curb depreciation – of technological and end products – would not affect private capital unequally. It would gradually modify the very concept of wealth by focusing on its content. Slower depreciation would allow better conservation of existing material wealth, both natural and humanly created. Slowing depreciation conserves the use value of existing wealth and fewer exchange values are realized. In other words, quantifiable wealth is no longer measured by its form. It is inventoried according to its use value, as wealth by-content. This new social bookkeeping gives priority to qualitative aspects over quantitative ones.

Realization of (practically) the same product recurs much less frequently when depreciation is regulated. Slower realization of profits on (practically) the same product will force capital to produce goods to satisfy unmet needs and/or previously neglected sectors of the population. Merely increasing the average period of depreciation for goods in the industrialized world by half would free more natural resources and energy than required to meet the needs of neglected sectors. This would entail reorganization of world demand and private sector income redistribution. Wealth by-content would grow rapidly to meet neglected sectors' needs and would simultaneously reduce consumption in 'over-served' groups. The common good of such regulated depreciation policies is evident. But how are private interests affected?

Slowing depreciation rates also decreases the now depleted mechanism for producing surplus value and profit rates. In the extreme case, the rate of depreciation can also cause average profit rates to drop and force capital to take refuge in the speculative sphere, throwing profits for the system as a whole into crisis. This new regulation would help maintain efficiency levels, although eventually it would drop in a smooth, controlled fashion in certain low-priority sectors and increase via the depreciation of more crucial use values for the citizenry as a whole.

Without eliminating the efficiency criterion, accentuating use values reaffirms the quality of wealth and life at the expense of the quantity of value produced. A revolution is not needed to make these changes in the economic rationality. By controlling the logic of accelerated depreciation and promoting its opposite, it is possible to conserve existing products. The difference between needs and wants becomes much clearer from this perspective. Use values and product quality gradually replace the desire to have things that are quantifiable numerically and by value. Value's content takes precedence, as does the quality of life, over consumerism. In other words, economic calculations are transformed.

For the *homo oeconomicus* 'needs' are unlimited and abstract. From the perspective of citizenry-based regulation they become more concrete and controllable. Unlimited wants emerge from the logic of perpetual creation of value and surplus value, and not from people's real needs. 'Unlimited needs' are a cultural value based on the ideal concept of wealth by-form. Once depreciation is regulated it is possible to control trends and channel investment to satisfy unmet needs. This rationality is driven by people's concrete needs and not by the private need for constant realization of value and surplus value.

This logic emphasizes the qualitative aspects of life including nature and the environment. The nature of social wealth and national bookkeeping changes. Meeting every person or citizen's basic needs now takes priority over per capita production and the growth of wealth. The primary focus shifts from the unbridled race to produce value and profits by meeting minority groups' artificial needs to ensuring the community's general quality of life (Roustang et al., 1996: 13, 42).

Towards citizen-based economic regulation Economic activity is organized around three basic aspects: the monetary mercantile or market economy; the nonmercantile monetary economy, including the welfare state's redistribution activities; and the nonmercantile nonmonetary economy that includes the barter of goods and services, and voluntary and domestic labour (Laville, 1994; Roustang et al., 1996: 66). Neoliberal political economy and Keynesianism have each favoured monetary aspects and marginalized unpaid labour regardless of its usefulness for the totality. Since neoclassical economics focuses on the remunerated parts – the market and the redistribution sphere – rather than the whole, it does not include unpaid work as labour.

Neoliberals have further limited economics by including the exclusionary logic of the market but not the state's redistribution activities (Maréchal, 1998: 19).

From the market economy perspective, we only exist and have purpose in so far as we exchange our labour force for money. According to the neoliberal view, social rights and citizenship originate in and are limited by exchange relations rather than in the totality. Chronically unemployed and marginalized sectors thus tend to be stripped of all rights. Citizen rights are not derived from membership in a society defined *a priori* as a nation or a people. We are members of society to the extent that we participate in its market. (Neo)liberal society is constructed from the parts and not the other way around.

According to this perspective, the existence of citizens' rights does not depend on membership in a nation or human community. They are created and destroyed within the confines of the market. We exist and have that right only as long as we exchange our labour (force) in the market. Those who do not are not considered part of that whole constructed from the parts. There is a tendency gradually to strip them of all social rights. The logic of globalization is exclusionary and those excluded tend to lose their ties to the market as well as their social rights. As more people never return to or even enter the market, this surplus population becomes a heavier burden for the market-based citizenry. Lacking ties to the market, they lose citizenship and no longer belong to the whole; they live instead at its expense. In a world where there is room for fewer and fewer citizens, those excluded represent a growing threat to the totality and tend to lose even the right to life. In other words, they are increasingly expendable. At its most extreme neoliberal logic can thus lead to neofascism (Forrester, 1996).

Neoliberals see the monetary-mercantile economy as the single real base of society. They question the Keynesian redistributive monetary economy, thus rejecting all citizen-based redistribution-led mediation (Roustang et al., 1996: 163). In Keynesian society, political debate on economic regulation from both left and right focused on the need for more or less government intervention in the monetary economy – mercantile and redistributive – and thus on a citizen-based reproductive logic. Employment policies were used to include more and broader sectors and expand social rights within the confines of the monetary economy. Beyond the monetary sphere, however, all unpaid labour – voluntary or domestic – was excluded and generally deprived of social rights.

By reconciling vitality and efficiency and protecting the latter, the Keynesian proposal entailed expanding involvement and income redistribution in function of increased demand and full employment as long as they did not conflict with profit rates. The social welfare state promoted a type of involvement aimed at making wage relations and citizenship more all-inclusive. It required economic growth and increased demand, which fuelled each other. Existence of widespread wage relations meant that the workforce was less replaceable, and so it became more important to protect it and provide it with better training. This in turn led to development of social rights and expansion of citizenship.

It became neoliberalism's task to salvage falling profit rates even at the expense of involvement, social rights, and thus of citizenship. The market economy is essentially exclusionary. Neoliberalism led to further deterioration of social rights and in the extreme to loss of citizenship and fundamental rights.

The new citizen-based economic regulation requires that these interests be inverted. Gradual subordination of private interests to the common good also inverts the notions of citizenship and the right to life. A project for society that places the citizenry above market relations is grounded in a concrete totality – a community of real human beings with real needs. In such a society, the citizenry is defined *a priori* and without exclusions: 'I no longer exist only so long as I exchange. I exist because we have decided with a social contract first and foremost to be a society' (Roustang et al., 1996: 163). These authors argue that now is the time to establish a social contract, but on a global rather than national scale. According to this world-citizen logic, all living beings on the planet possess the right to life, which is not exclusive to those participating in the market. Rights are not tied to the exchange of labour. Labour itself is every citizen's right, as is the right to life. Its citizen base and the right to life are the principal arenas in which to develop this alternative that embraces both included and excluded sectors.

From the totality-centred perspective, labour and wealth are not restricted to the market or to the monetary realm. Given the market economy's long history, it is not easy or quick to invert these axes, but under regulated depreciation social bookkeeping tends to focus more on labour's content and less on its form. In this new economic rationality, market and monetary relations become part of the totality but their sum total does not equal the whole. Nonquantifiable voluntary and domestic labour and (the conservation of) nature all contribute to the reproduction of the whole. The new social bookkeeping includes the contributions made by the parts to the reproduction of the whole, but not the inverse. It is not a matter of putting a price on domestic labour and nature or increasing the sum of the parts. This approach is more qualitative than quantitative. The logic of the simple sum of the parts involved in exchange is replaced with a different type of economic calculations. Just as life is defined more in terms of quality of life and less as 'life expectancy' or quantity of life, social bookkeeping is becoming more qualitative and focusing more on quality of life.

Global economic regulation and the state Under totality-based economic regulation, competitive advantage is no longer the main priority. Market-based integration of the world stems from the parts and ends up destroying the whole. The parts cannot be the starting point from which to achieve the common good. Globalization favours the competitive advantage of the parts in the market. A citizen-based approach involves suppressing these competitive advantages and leads to deglobalization: 'The debate over necessary economic and social regulation of globalization can only proceed after accepting that deglobalization is needed' (Fouquet and Lemaître, 1997: 162). Real citizen-based economic regulation, where transnational private interests are subordinated to those of the citizenry, must be developed on a worldwide scale. Only such global economic regulation can subordinate global free market competitive advantage. The fundamental task is not to change globalization as such, but to change its content and its basis.

Petrella has stated that ending neoliberal globalization requires 'declaring general economic disarmament to end the Economic World War' (Petrella, 1996: 13). Doubts about deregulation of the world economy multiply both from above and below, as the cracks in neoliberalism become more evident. Reglobalization is a purely political worldwide endeavour. Decisions must be made by those in power, but pressure by the world citizenry is needed for that power to act, as occurred with the MAI initiative. Formal political power is held by the G-7 – or G-8 when including Russia – and the 29 OECD member nations. That is where most transnational corporations and real economic power are concentrated.

No single nation-state can regulate transnational corporations' global activities and it is increasingly difficult for nation-states acting together as well. As the cracks in neoliberalism have become more apparent even developed countries have been losing autonomy. This represents an opportunity to develop greater awareness throughout the planet about the possibility of global regulation. Responding to pressure by the world citizenry many of those agencies created and used to promote economic deregulation – such as the IMF, the WTO, and the MAI – can continue by changing their objectives to include global economic regulation. This was actually the original purpose of those oldest agencies. Such a shift is not impossible, but it does require the worldwide political will that can only occur when large transnational corporations' profits are seriously endangered. Global regulation requires adequate governability (Fouquet and Lemaître, 1997: 162), which means reducing the power of nation-states to deregulate national and international economies and helping them to re-regulate.

Different authors have thus presented proposals for global, national and regional intervention (Petrella, 1996; Fouquet and Lemaître, 1997; Roustang et al., 1996; Cassen, 1998). Cassen (1998: 11) argued for a true MAI based on citizens' rights and investors' obligations. Others have proposed worldwide regulation of the environment (collective resource management), employment (worldwide employment policies and global collective agreements), and social protection (worldwide social security) to benefit the citizenry (Fouquet and Lemaître, 1997: 176–9). Many others could be mentioned, but none has advocated regulated depreciation on a global scale as a means of changing the essential economic rationality without suppressing private interests.

The philosophy of the social welfare state comes up short in this new context. Totality-based economic regulation requires new articulation of nation-states and world governability, on the one hand, and of the citizenry and state intervention on the other. Subordination of nation-states to world governability must be citizen-based instead of primarily serving private interests. This logic and rationality portray a solidarity state (Roustang et al., 1996: 172). It is citizen-based and can achieve true democratic participation and progressive involvement in the allocation of social production and of wealth in general. Compared to the social welfare state, it must balance more areas of the economy. This totality-based reproductive logic focuses on the non-monetary economy – nature and unpaid labour – as well as the monetary economy – the redistributive and market economies. This entails direct participation by the solidarity state in world environmental conservation projects grounded in a solidarity ethic. The domestic sphere must also be considered a central part of society (Maréchal, 1998: 19).

The Subject in a Citizen-based Globalization

This is a crucial moment in history. The cracks in neoliberalism are more and more evident and uncertainty of economic stability is spreading around the globe. In a world with room for fewer and fewer people or transnational companies, this could lead to increased aggression with neofascist overtones around the world. As more widespread exclusion fosters increasingly aggressive accumulation, future scenarios could even include development of a war economy. It could not provide long-term solutions, even for the victors, since the increasingly aggressive economy tends to abandon vitality. Sooner or later, it must be rechannelled towards global economic re-regulation. To develop an alternative capable of averting this extreme radical neoliberalism requires a broad-based front that places citizenry and vitality ahead of private interests and efficiency. A world citizenry conscious of the need to put the totality ahead of private interests is the key to any real solution. Globalization thus creates the objective conditions so that the greatest possible number of actors can join together on a single stage to formulate the future human society that we all desire (Guibernau, 1996: 145).

Any specific alternative assumes and generates a specific subject. Neoliberalism created the *homo oeconomicus* that operates according to a market rationality and based on increasingly unmediated individual interests. A decline in solidarity has followed this subject's development. Extreme neoliberalism results in a society where only the 'fittest' have a real right to life. The legitimacy of this survival of the fittest prevails as society becomes more exclusionary.

Citizenry and social rights in a market economy are determined by their place in the market and within its confines. World citizens having better market positions are fuller citizens enjoying more rights, including the right to a more developed life. Where there is widespread structural exclusion, such as in peripheral countries, citizenry is much less developed, as are social rights and the right to and respect for life itself. A crisis of citizenry has emerged in this world that has room for increasingly few, giving rise to concerted efforts in their defence. In the last and extreme instance, 'first-class citizens' are threatened with increasing exclusion and feel they have more right to be in this world. History has shown that, in the extreme, they begin to define the lives of the growing mass of 'second-class citizens' who lack all structural ties to the market as well as social rights or even the right to life. Since the right to life is determined by market position and not the other way around, extreme neoliberalism can actually lead to neofascism and the development of a historical subject who, as Forrester has argued (1997), can justify an eventual shift from exclusion to systematic elimination of the surplus population.

True socialism intended to eliminate the market and private interest in favour of a Common Good-centred reproductive logic. The centralized plan replaced the total market as the central focus of economic rationality. The suppressed market made it difficult to reconcile the Common Good and virtually stifled private interests. As a result, the Common Good is defined from above – for the citizenry but without their participation. The plan by which to achieve this was vertically formulated and executed by a party bureaucracy. Their ties to the citizenry were lost when their ties with private interest were broken. Market totalitarianism is thus replaced by the absolutism of the plan.

The historical subject that aimed to implement real socialism anticipated this rationality as an exclusionary and vertical vanguard. It was defined according to social relations of exploitation – the working class. The more a sector of workers was excluded from the market, the less important they were as potential working-class allies and participants in the revolutionary project. In fact, this notion is not citizen-based. Its historical subject, defined by the same market relations it is attempting to eliminate, itself defines the new society to be built for the citizenry.

Conciliation of private interests and the Common Good allows and requires greater democratic participation by citizens. Following increased and more widespread levels of involvement, the logic of the social welfare state has allowed the working class greater participation in decision-making and allocation of social production. This generalization of wage relations led to expansion of the citizenry and not the other way around. In a market economy, women's struggle for equality, for example, is only successful inasmuch as they participate in wage relations. As wage labour becomes more widespread the social welfare state expands and their involvement in decision-making and allocation of social production increases.

There were limits to this involvement and to democratic participation under the social welfare state. Full democracy must be truly citizen-based and not centred ultimately on private interests. Democratization along with the social welfare state reached its limits as soon as profit rates fell. The only way to expand participatory democracy was to invert the relationship between private interest and the citizenry. Under the social welfare state, citizen rights were determined by the fact that most of the active-age population was included in wage relations and in function of capital, but not by their membership in the totality. Rights derived from non-wage and non-monetary labour – domestic and volunteer labour – served no apparent purpose for capital, regardless of its contribution to vitality, and was very restricted.

Under the social welfare state, participation in decision-making and allocation of social production can expand only so far as it does not conflict with efficiency. Increased citizen participation is possible only as long as expanding involvement and citizenship continues to favour private interests and efficiency. The battle to protect private interests at all costs kicks off the moment profit rates fall, revealing a drop in efficiency. This leads to the reduction of involvement, participation and democracy, as occurred with neoliberalism's expansion since the 1970s.

The alternative historical project proposes inverting the relationship between private interests and the common good, ultimately favouring the whole. Totality-based projects are centred on the citizenry in its natural surroundings. Social rights and the right to life are derived from membership in the human community and not limited by participation in the market or to its confines. This project would not abolish the market, but would gradually subordinate its rationality to that of the citizenry. In other words, it would intercede between private interests and the common good in favour of the latter. It essentially aims to invert economic rationality to favour the citizenry instead of private interests. It is highly inclusive and does not *a priori* exclude any sector. Consensus-building is the primary method for reaching these objectives and any form of violence is reserved only for the most extreme circumstances of last resort. The international movement against the MAI represents a first step in this direction. The ethic of solidarity with all citizens' real lives is the foundation on which this historical subject is building a postcapitalist alternative to neoliberalism.

Economic regulation: Common Good and private interests The new economic regulations must be totality-centred rather than focusing on the private parties with conflicting interests. This in turn transforms the economic rationality. It is no longer sufficient that a visible hand guide the invisible one, while still leaving free market forces the last word. Intervention is needed on behalf of the Common Good, along with elimination of preferences given to competitive advantage in the free market. Consequently, inefficiency and protectionism must be re-evaluated when they are used to further the Common Good.

From the perspective of the whole, free market forces result in bankruptcies and therefore lead to massive capital destruction and loss of jobs, as well as economic stagnation, environmental destruction and the widespread loss of future jobs and development opportunities, all just to safeguard transnational profits (Roustang et al., 1996: 36). Inverting this rationality and declaring what Petrella (1996: 13) has called worldwide economic disarmament can finally bring the economic world war to an end.

We have a historic opportunity to formulate a real MAI based on the rights of citizens in investment recipient countries and the obligations of investors. It would include unconditional respect for existing or future social and environmental norms. It would also require that a given percentage of the aggregate value be created locally, a portion of the products be sold on site, and a share of the profits be reinvested. Public outlays must be repaid with interest and companies abandoning the country would incur stiff financial penalties (Cassen, 1998: 11).

Economic rationality is determined by which economic performance criteria are defined as priorities by a society at a given time in history. The real problem with neoliberalism lies not in the economy itself but in the exercise of political control over it. Likewise, inverting the global economic rationality is a political, not economic, issue. This same economic globalization also provides the possibility and even the historical need to subordinate micro-level efficiency to macro-level vitality. By reclaiming the Common Good it becomes possible to transcend the nationalism of the past and, for the first time in history, to function on behalf of humanity as a whole (CASPCCJ, 1997: 5).

Bibliography

Adda, J. (1994) 'Développement au-delà de l'ajustement', *L'Economie Mondiale*, Paris: La Découverte, pp. 78–96.

Aglietta, M. (1979) *Regulación y crisis del capitalismo*, Mexico City: Siglo XXI.

Aguirre, M. and G. Malgesini (eds) (1991) *Misiles o microchips: la conversión de la industria militar en civil*, Barcelona: ICARIA.

Alber, J. (1982) *Von Armenhaus zum Woliljahrtaat*, Frankfurt: Campus.

Altvater, E. and F. Feerkhuizen (1978) 'Sobre el trabajo productivo e improductivo', *Crítica de la economía política*, 8, Mexico: El Caballito.

Amin, S. (1996) *Les Défits de la mondialisation*, Paris: Harmattan.

Anderson, P. (1996) 'Balance del neoliberalismo: lecciones para la izquierda', *El Rodaballo* (Spain), January.

Andreff, W. (1995) *Les Multinationales globales*, Paris: La Découverte.

Barahona, A. (1997) 'Pero, qué es la globalización', *Hombres de Maíz*, VII (46) (March–April): 4–6.

Baran, P. A. and P. M. Sweezy (1966) *Monopoly Capital*, New York: Monthly Review Press

Barbú, Z. (1970) 'El fascismo europeo: Rumania', in S. J. Woolf (ed.), *El fascismo europeo*, Mexico: Grijalbo, pp. 144–62.

Beckerman, W. (1972) 'Economists, scientists and environmental catastrophe', *Oxford Economic Papers*, November.

Benoit, E. (1973) *Defense and Economic Growth in Developing Countries*, Toronto: Lexington Books.

Beulens, F. (1995) 'De wereld handelsorganizatie en de sociale clausules', *International Spectator*, 49 (10) (October).

Bifani, P. (1980) *Medio y medio ambiente*, Madrid: CIFCA.

Bonefeld, W. (1995) 'Dinero y libertad, el poder constitutivo del trabajo y la reproducción capitalista', in J. Holloway et al., *Globalización y Estados-nación: el monetarismo en la crisis actual*, Buenos Aires: Tierra y Fuego.

Bonefeld, W. and J. Holloway (1995) 'Dinero y lucha de clases', in J. Holloway et al., *Globalización y Estados-nación: el monetarismo en la crisis actual*, Buenos Aires: Tierra y Fuego.

Braudel, F. (1991) *La identidad de Francia*, Barcelona: Gidsa.

Buelens, F. (1995) 'De wereldhandelsorganizatie en de sociale clausules', *Internationale Spectator*, 49 (10) (October).

Caillé, A. (1997) '30 thèses pour contribuer à l'émergence d'une gauche nouvelle et universalisable', *La Revue du MAUSS Semestrelle*, 9 (1st semester): 297–31.

Camilleri, J. (1992) *The End of Sovereignty: The Politics of a Shrinking and Fragmenting World*, Adershot: Edward Elger.

Campanario, P. and W. Dierckxsens (1984) 'E papel de la superpoblación relativa en el reformismo en Costa Rica', *Revista Entroamericana de Economía* (Honduras), 5 (14).

CASPCCJ (Comisión de Apostolado Social de la Provincia Centroamericana de la Compañía de Jesús) (1997) 'Compromiso hacia una nueva sociedad. Opción en tiempos de globalización', *Pasos* (Costa Rica), 71 (May–June): 1–10.

Cassen, B. (1998) 'Les dix commandements de la préférence citoyenne', *Le Monde Diplomatique* (May): 10–11.

CEPII (Centro de Investigaciones para la Paz) (1989) *Anuario 1988–1989*, Madrid: IEPALA.

— (1994) *L'Economie mondiale 1995*, Paris: La Découverte.

— (1996) *Economía mundial 1990–2000: el imperativo del crecimiento*, Buenos Aires: Corregidor.

Chalmers, J. et al. (1989) *The Politics of Productivity*, Cambridge, MA: Ballinger Books.

Chesnais, F. (1998) 'La face financière d'une crise de surproduction', *Le Monde Diplomatique* (February): 18.

Chomsky, N. and H. Dietrich (1995) *La sociedad global*, Mexico City: Contrapuntos.

Cleaver, H. (1995) 'La subversión del patrón dinero en la crisis actual', in J. Holloway et al., *Globalización y Estados-nación: el monetarismo en la crisis actual*, Buenos Aires: Tierra y Fuego.

Closkey, H. (1988) *Etica y política de la ecología*, Mexico City: Fondo de Cultura Económica.

Coutrot, T. (1998) *L'Entreprise néolibérale: nouvelle utopie capitaliste?* Paris: La Découverte.

Deger, S. (1985) 'Does defense expenditure mobilise resources?', *Journal of Economic Studies*, 12 (4): 15–29.

Dierckxsens, W. (1979) *Capitalismo y poblaceón*, San José: DEI.

— (1983) *Formaciones Precapitalistas*, San José: EDUCA.

— (1990) *Mercado de trabajo y política económica en América Central*, San José: DEI.

— (1992) *Globalización: Centroamérica y el Caribe en el nuevo orden*, San José: CCC-CA.

— (1994) *De la globalización a la Perestroika occidental*, San José: DEI.

— (1995) *Ascenso y caída de la seguridad social en América Latina: globalización, desarrollo humano y transición demográfica*, internal document, IVO, University of Tilberg, the Netherlands.

— (1997) 'Globalización y economía de casino', *Pasos* (Costa Rica), 70 (March–April): 1–26.

Donahue, T. (1994) 'International labour standards: the perspective of labour', *International Labour Standards and Global Economic Integration*, Washington, DC: US Department of Labor (July).

Downs, A. (1973) 'The political economy of improving our environment', in J. Bain, *Environment Decay*, Boston, MA: Little, Brown.

Drucker, P. (1994) *La sociedad postcapitalista*, Barcelona: Norma.

Dunning, J. (1992) 'The global economy, domestic governance, stategies and transnational corporations', *Transnational Corporations* (UN), 1 (3) (December): 7–46.

Economist, The (1996) *The World in 1997*, London: The Economist.

Engelhard, P. (1996) *L'Homme mondial: les sociétés humaines peuvent-elles survivre?* Paris: Arléa.

— (1997) *La troisième guerre mondiale a commencé*, Paris: Arléa.

Enkins, P. (1989) 'Trade and reliance', *The Ecologist*, 119 (5).

Enzenberger, M. (1974) 'Contribucion a la crítica de la ecología política', *Siempre* (Mexico), 633–4.

Espinoza, R. (1996) *Hacia una Nueva Sociedad en Mexico con lugar para todos*, San José: Investigation Advance at DEI.

Ezcurra, A. M. (1997) 'Globalización, neoloberalismo y sociedad civil. Algunos desafíos para los movimentos sociales y populares latinoamericanos', *Pasos* (Costa Rica), 71 (May–June): 17–30.

Faini, R., P. Annez and L. Taylor (1984) 'Defense spending, economic structure and growth: evidence among countries and over time', *Economic Development and Cultural Change*, 32 (3) (April): 487–98.

Fallows, J. (1993) 'Looking at the sun', *Atlantic Monthly*, 272 (5).

Feldstein, I. (1998) 'Refocusing the FMI', *Foreign Affairs* (March): 20–33.

Fiorito, R. (1974) *División de Trabajo y Teoría del Valor*, Comunicación Serie B, Madrid: Felmar.

FMI (1998) *Boletin*, 27 (1) (January): 1–2.

Forrester, V. (1997) *El horror económico*, Mexico F.D.: Fondo de Cultura Económica.

Fouquet, A. and F. Lemaître (1997) *Démystifier la mondialisation de l'économie*, Paris: Les Editions de l'Organisation.

Fox, J. (1998) 'Can the US economy hold up?' *Fortune*, 28 September, pp. 49–54.

Freeman, R. (1994) *A Global Labour Market: Differences in Wages among Countries in the 1980s*, Washington, DC: World Bank.

Fukuyama, F. (1995) *Welvaart: de grondslagen van het economisch handelen*, Amsterdam: Contact.

Galbraith, J. K. (1995) *Wereldeconomie in deze eeuw*, Baarn, the Netherlands: SESAM.

Goldsmith, E. (1996) 'Quand les firmes transnacionales imposent leur loi', *Le Monde Diplomatique* (April): 9.

Gombeaud, J.-L. and M. Décaillot (1997) *Le Retour de la très grande dépression*, Paris: Economica.

González Butrón, M. A. (1997) 'Desde el mundo de las excluidas para un mundo donde quepan todos y todos: por un visibilización de las invisibles', *Pasos* (Costa Rica), 70 (March–April): 50–82.

Goodmann, J. and L. Pauly (1993) 'The obsolescence of capital controls', *World Politics*, 46 (1): 50–82.

Gough, I. (1997) 'Gastos del estado en el capitalismo avanzado', in H. Sontag and H. Valecillos (eds), *El Estado en el capitalismo contemporáneo*, Mexico City: Siglo XXI, pp. 224–302.

— (1978) 'La teoría del trabajo productivo e improductivo en Marx', *Crítica de la Economía Política*, 8, Mexico: El Caballito.

Gray, J. (1998) *False Dawn: The Delusion of Global Capitalism*, London: Granta.

Gréau, J.-L. (1998) *Le Capitalisme malade de sa finance*, Paris: Gallimard.

Greg, I. (1997) 'Un lunes sangriento para los mercados bursátiles mundiales', *The Wall Street Journal Americas*, supplement to *La Nación*, San José, 28 October, p. 25A.

Guibernau, M. (1996) *Los nacionalismos*, Barcelona: Ariel.

Gutiérrez, G. (1997) 'Etica funcional y ética de la vida', *Pasos* (Costa Rica), 74 (November–December): 15–25.

Gutman, P. (1986) 'Economía y ambiente', in E. Leff (ed.), *Los problemas del conocimiento y la perspectiva ambiental del desarrollo*, Mexico City: Siglo XXI.

Harrison, J. (1974) 'Political economy of housework', *Bulletin of the Conference of Socialist Economists* (Spring).

Hayek, F. (1989) 'El ideal democrático y la contención del poder', (Chile), 1 (December).

— (1992) *Sobre la libertad*, San José: Libro Libre.

Heilbroner, R. (1992) *Kapitalisme in de 21ste eeuw*, Amsterdam: Van Gennep.

Heise, A. (1996) 'Der Mythos con Sachzwang Weltmarkt', *Politik und Gesellschaft* (Bonn: Dietz Verlag), 1: 17–22.

Hinkelhammert, F. (1984) *Crítica a la razón utópica*, San José: DEI.

— (1995) *Cultura de la esperanza y sociedad sin exclusión*, San José: DEI.

— (1996) 'Determinismo y autoconstitución del sujeto. Las leyes que se imponen a espaldas de los actores y el orden por el desorden', *Pasos*, 64 (March–April): 18–31.

— (1997) 'El huracán de la globalizacieon', *Pasos*, 69 (January–February): 21–7.

— (1997a) 'El asesinato es un suicidio: de la utilidad de la limitación del cálculo de utilidad', *Pasos*, 74 (November–December): 26–37.

Holloway, J. and W. Bonefeld (1995) *Globalización y Estados-natión*, Buenos Aires: Tierra y Fuego.

Huber, P. (1994) *Orwell's Revenge: The 1984 Palimpsest*, New York: Free Press.

Huntington, S. (1993) 'The clash of civilizations', *Foreign Affairs* (Summer): 32–50.

— *The Clash of Civilizations and the Remaking of the World Order*, New York: Simon and Schuster.

Ianni, O. (1996) *Teorías de globalización*, Mexico City: Siglo XXI.

ILO (1993) *El empleo en el mundo*, Geneva: ILO.

— (1995) *El empleo en el mundo*, Geneva: ILO.

— (1996) *El empleo en el mundo 1996/1997: las políticas nacionales en una era de la mundialización*, Geneva: ILO.

— (1997) *La actividad normativa de la OITen la era de la mundialización*, Geneva: ILO.

— (1999) *Informe sobre el empleo en el mundo 1998–1999*, Geneva: ILO.

IMF (1998) *IMF Bulletin*, 27 (1) (January): 1–2.

IRELA (1996) *La Unión Europea y el Grupo de Río: la agenda birregional 1990–1995*, Madrid: IRELA.

Isuani, E. A. (1986) 'Seguridad social y asistencia pública', in C. Mesa-Lago, *La crisis de seguridad social y la atención a la salud*, Mexico: Fondo de Cultura Económica.

Julien, C. (1996) 'Une Europe des citoyens', *Le Monde Diplomatique* (March/April).

Keynes, J. M. (1936) *The General Theory of Employment, Interest and Money*, London: Macmillan.

Kolo, G. (1998) 'De la faillité des dogmes: mais exportez donc! dit le FMI', *Le Monde Diplomatique* (May): 7.

Korsh, K. (1982) *Escritos políticos*, Mexico City: Folios.

Kozlik, A. (1968) *El capitalismo del desperdicio*, Mexico City: Siglo XXI.

Kraft, M. (1977) 'Political change and sustainable society', in D. Pirages (ed.), *The Sustainable Society*, New York: Praeger, pp. 173–96.

Krusewitz, K. (1978) 'Opmerking over de oorzaken van de milieukrisis in historie-maatschappelijke samenhang', in H. Verhagen (ed.), *Inleiding tot de politieke ekonomie van liet milieu*, Amsterdam: Ekologische Uitgeverij, pp. 81–109.

Laville, J.-L. (1994) *L'Economie solidaire: une perspective internationale*, Paris: Desclée de Brouwer.

— (1997) 'Une politique économique pour le XXI siècle', *La Revue du MAUSS Semestrelle*, 9 (1st semester): 243–7.

Lawrence, R. (1992) 'Japan's low levels of inward investment: the role of inhibitions and acquisitions', *Transnational Corporations*, 1 (3) (December).

Leff, E. (1986) *Ecología y capital: hacía una perspectiva ambiental del desarrollow*, Mexico City: Universidad Autónoma de México.

Lennep, E. van (1995) 'Nederland in een veranderende economische wereldorde', *Internationale Spectator* (The Hague), 49 (10) (October): 507–13.

Lipietz, A. (1995) 'El mundo del postfordismo', *Utopías* (Madrid), 166 (October–December).

Lula-da Silva, L. I. (1997) 'Sindicalistas del mundo, unios', *Hombres de Maíz* (Costa Rica), VII (46) (March–April): 18–19.

McHarg, I. (1969) *Design with Nature*, New York: Natural History Press.

Maddison, A. (1996) *Problemas del crecimiento económico de las naciones*, Mexico City: Planeta Mexicana.

Mandel, E. (1972) *Tratado de economía marxista*, Mexico City: Era.

— (1976) *Het laatkapitalisme*, Amsterdam: Van Gennep.

Maréchal, J.-P. (1998) 'Imaginer une autre société: demain l'économie solidaire', *Le Monde Diplomatique* (April): 1–19.

Margolin, J.-L. (1994) 'L'Asie Orientale, de la prosperité à l'unité', in CEPII, *L'Economie Mondiale 1995*, Paris: La Découverte, pp. 87–96.

Marshal, A. (1981) *El mercado de trabajo en el capitalismo periférico*, Mexico City: El Colegio de México.

Martin, H.-P. and H. Schumann (1996) *Die globalisierungsfalle: Der Angriff auf Demokratie und Wohlstand*, Hamburg: Rowohlt; (English trans 1997) *The Global Trap: Globalization and the Assault on Prosperity and Democracy*, London: Zed Books.

Marx, K. (1973) *El Capital: crítica de la economía política*, Buenos Aires: Cartago.

— (1974) *Teorías sobre la plusvalía*, Buenos Aires: Cartago.

Meiksins Wood, E. (1997) 'Back to Marx', *Monthly Review*, 49 (2) (June): 1–17.

Melman, S. (1991) 'El imperativo de la conversión económica. Once proposiciones', in M. Aguirre and G. Malgesini (eds), *Misiles o microchips: la conversión de la industria militar en civil*, Barcelona: ICARIA, pp. 43–66.

Mesa-Lago, C. (ed.) *La crisis de la seguridad social y la atención a la salud*, Mexico City: Fondo de Cultura Económica.

— (1990) *La seguridad social y el sector informal*, Chile: PREALC/OIT.

Mier, S. (1997) 'Conformación de la sociedad civil como sujeto social y ético', *Teología y Ciencias Humanas* (Mexico), LXII (May–June): 51–3.

Millán, J. (1992) *La Cuenca del Pacifico*, Mexico City: Fondo de Cultura Económica.

Miliman, G. (1995) *De nieuwe geldwolven*, Utrecht: Scheffers.

Molas Gallart, J. (1991) 'Aproximación a los aspectos económicos de la defensa', in M. Aguirre and G. Melgesini (eds), *Misiles o microchips: la conversión de la industria militar en civil*, Barcelona: ICARIA, pp. 339–98.

Moon, B. (1996) *Dilemmas of International Trade*, Boulder, CO: Westview Press.

Morin, E. (1980) *La Méthode, la vie de la vie*, Paris: Editions du Seuil.

Morrison, A. and K. Roth (1992) 'The regional solution: an alternative to globalization', *Transnational Corporations*, 1 (2) (August): 37–56.

Mortimer, E. (1997) 'Global gloom', *Financial Times*, 25 March, p. 14.

NACLA (1997) special issue 'Report on the Americas: Latin America in the Age of Billionaires', XXX (6) (May–June).

Nadal Egea, A. (1991) *Arsenales nucleares: tecnología decadente y control de armamentos*, Mexico City: Colegio de México.

Nell, E. J. (1996) *Making Sense of a Changing Economy*, London: Routledge.

Ngoc Liem, H. (1998) *La Facture sociale: sommes-nous condemnés au libéralisme?* Paris: Arléa.

Nocera, J. (1998) 'Requiem for the bull', *Fortune* (September): 40–3.

OECD (1995) *Perspectives économiques de l'OCDE*, Paris: OECD (June).

Ohmae, K. (1996) *The End of the Nation State*, New York: Free Press.

OIT (1993) *El empleo en el mundo*, Geneva: OIT.

— (1995) *El empleo en el mundo*, Geneva: OIT.

— (1996) *El empleo en el mundo. 1996–97: Las políticas nacionales en una era de mundialización*, Geneva: OIT.

— (1997) *La actividad normativa de la OIT en la era de la mundialización*, Geneva: OIT.

ONU (1992, 1993) *Transnational Corporations*, New York: ONU.

Ormerod, P. (1995) *Economen hebben geen idee*, Amsterdam: Van Lennep.

Osa, A. de la (1996) 'Cuenca del Caribe: mecanismos para profundizar la participación de los actores sociales en el proceso de regionalización', paper presented at the international seminar 'La Nueva Agenda Socio-política del Proceso de Integración en el Gran Caribe', Caracas: INVESP, February.

Ostry, S. (1992) 'Domain: the new international policy arena', in *Transnational Corporations* (New York: United Nations), 1 (3): 1–27.

Paz, P. (1983) 'Crisis financiera internacional, neoliberalismo y respuestas nacionales', in M. Ramírez et al., *Banca y crisis del sistema*, Mexico City: Pueblo Nuevo.

Pearce, D. (1985) *Economía ambiental*, Mexico City: Fondo de Cultura Económica.

Petrella, R. (1996) 'Competitiveness and the need for economic disarmament', *Politik und Gesellschaft* (Bonn: Dietz Verlag), 1: 7–16.

Porter, M. (1990) *La ventaja comparativa de las naciones*, Buenos Aires: Vergara.

Prestowitz, C. (1988) *Trading Places: How We All Allowed Japan to Take the Lead*, New York: Basic Books.

Quaini, M. (1977) *Marxisme en Geografie*, Amsterdam: Ecologische Uitgeverij.

Quesnay, F. (1958) *Tableau Economique*, Mexico City: Fondo de Cultura Económica.

Ramonet, I. (1997a) *Un mundo sin rumbo: crisis de fin de siglo*, Madrid: Debate.

— (1997b) 'Régimes globalitaires', *Le Monde Diplomatique* (January): 1.

— (1998) 'Un autre monde est possible, besoin de utopie', *Le Monde Diplomatique* (May): 9.

Reich, R. (1993) *El trabajo de las naciones*, Buenos Aires: Vergara.

Revista del Sur (Montevideo) (1988), 78 (April).

Rifkin, J. (1997) *The End of Work: The Decline of the Global Labour Force and the Dawn of the Post Market Era*, New York: G.P. Putnam's Sons.

Rodrik, D. (1995) 'Labour standards and international trade: moving beyond the rhetoric' (mimeo), Washington, DC: Overseas Development Council (June).

Rohwer, J. (1998) 'Why the global storm will zap the US economy', *Fortune*, 28 September, pp. 22–3.

Rousseau, J. J. (1950) *The Social Contract and Discourses*, New York: Dutton.

Roustang, G. and J.-L. Laville (1996) *Vers un nouveau contrat social*, Paris: Declée de Brouwer.

Sachs, J. (1998) 'Global capitalism: making it work', *The Economist*, 12–18 September, pp. 21–2.

Sapford, D. and J. Williams (1997) 'La cronología del desastre asiático', *The Wall Street Journal Americas*, supplement to *El Comercio Ecterior*, Quito, 27 November.

Schmidt, A. (1976) *El concepto de Naturaleza en Marx*, Mexico City: Siglo XXI.

Sender, H. (1997) 'Not a happy bunch', *Economic Review*, 2 October.

Sewell, W. and P. Sutherland (1998) *The Challenges of Globalization*, Washington, DC: Overseas Development Council.

Shaw, A. (1991) 'La conversión y los problemas económico-sociales surgidos de las políticas de desarme', in M. Aguirre and G. Melgesini (eds), *Misiles o microchips: la conversión de la industria militar en civil*, Barcelona: ICARIA, pp. 67–96.

Shutt, H. (1998) *The Trouble with Capitalism: Global Economic Failure*, London: Zed Books.

Singer, P. (1980) *Economia política del trabajo*, Mexico City: Siglo XXI.

Smith, A. (1975) *The Theory of Moral Sentiments*, Oxford: Oxford University Press.

Sweezy, P. (1970) *Teoría del desarrollo económico*, Mexico City: Fondo de Cultura Económico.

Tabb, W. (1997) 'Globalization as an issue: the power of capital as the issue', *Monthly Review* (June): 20–30.

Taylor, G. R. (1970) *The Doomsday Book*, London: Panther.

Thurow, L. (1992) *La Guerra del siglo XXI*, Buenos Aires: Vergara.

— (1996) *The Future of Capitalism*, New York: Vergara.

Tobin, J. (1978) 'A proposal for an international monetary reform', *Eastern Economic Journal*, 3/4 (July/October).

Tyson, L. (1993) *Who is Bashing Whom: Trade Conflicts in High Technology Industries*, Institute for International Economics.

UNCTAD Division for Transnational Corporations (1998) *Transnational Corporations in World Development*, New York: UNCTAD.

— (1993) *World Investment Report*, New York: UNCTAD.

— (1999) *World Investment Report*, New York: UNCTAD.

UNDP (1992) *Human Development Report 1992*, Oxford and New York: Oxford University Press.

Verhagen, H. (1978) *Inleiding tot de politieke ekonomie van het milieu*, Amsterdam: Ekologische Uitgeverij.

Vidal, D. (1998) 'Dans le sud, développement ou régression?', *Le Monde Diplomatique* (October): 26.

Wallerstein, I. (1989) *El capitalismo histórico*, Mexico City: Siglo XXI.

— (1991) *The Politics of the World Economy*, Cambridge: Cambridge University Press.

Wesselius, E. (1998) 'Het multilateraal akkoord inzake investeringen', *Solidariteit* (February): 9.

West, R. (1991) 'La economía militar y el problema del desarrollo en los países del Tercer Mundo', in M. Aguirre and G. Malgesini (eds) *Misiles o microchips: la conversión de la industria militar en civil*, Barcelona: ICARIA, pp. 399–504.

Wolf, M. (1997) 'Mais pourquoi cette haine des marchés?, *Le Monde Diplomatique* (June): 14–15.

Zevin, R. (1992) *Our Financial Market is More Open: If So, Why and with What Effect?*, New York: Oxford University Press.

Index

Zed Titles on Globalization

Globalization has become the new buzzword of the late 1990s. Despite the very different meanings attached to the term and even more divergent evaluations of its likely impacts, it is clear nevertheless that we are in an accelerated process of transition to a new period in world history. Zed Books' titles on globalization pay special attention to what it means for the South, for women, for workers and for other vulnerable groups.

Nassau Adams, *Worlds Apart: The North–South Divide and the International System*

Samir Amin, *Capitalism in the Age of Globalization: The Management of Contemporary Society*

Asoka Bandarage, *Women, Population and Global Crisis: A Political-Economic Analysis*

Michel Chossudovsky, *The Globalisation of Poverty: Impacts of IMF and World Bank Reforms*

Peter Custers, *Capital Accumulation and Women's Labour in Asian Economies*

Bhagirath Lal Das, *An Introduction to the WTO Agreements*

Bhagirath Lal Das, *The WTO Agreements: Deficiencies, Imbalances and Required Changes*

Bhagirath Lal Das, *The World Trade Organization: A Guide to the New Framework for International Trade*

Diplab Dasgupta, *Structural Adjustment, Global Trade and the New Political Economy of Development*

Graham Dunkley, *The Free Trade Adventure: The WTO, GATT and Globalism: A Critique*

Bjorn Hettne et al., *International Political Economy: Understanding Global Disorder*

Terence Hopkins and Immanuel Wallerstein et al., *The Age of Transition: Trajectory of the World-System, 1945–2025*

Jomo, K. S. (ed.), *Tigers in Trouble: Financial Governance, Liberalisation and the Economic Crises in East Asia*

Hans-Peter Martin and Harald Schumann, *The Global Trap: Globalization and the Assault on Prosperity and Democracy*

Harry Shutt, *The Trouble with Capitalism: An Enquiry into the Causes of Global Economic Failure*

Kavaljit Singh, *The Globalisation of Finance: A Citizen's Guide*

Henk Thomas (ed.), *Globalization and Third World Trade Unions*

Christa Wichterich, *The Globalized Woman: Reports from a Future of Inequality*

David Woodward, *Foreign Direct and Equity Investment in Developing Countries: The Next Crisis?*

For full details of this list and Zed's other subject and general catalogues, please write to:

The Marketing Department, Zed Books, 7 Cynthia Street, London N1 9JF, UK or e-mail: sales@zedbooks.demon.co.uk